# Signs and Seasons

Graham Kings is the vicar of St Mary's Islington, one of London's most vibrant churches. He is co-founder and theological secretary of Fulcrum, a leading evangelical organization in the Church of England and the Anglican Communion.

# Signs and Seasons

*A guide for your Christian journey*

Graham Kings

CANTERBURY
PRESS
Norwich

First published in 2008 by the Canterbury Press Norwich
(a publishing imprint of Hymns Ancient & Modern Limited,
a registered charity)
13–17 Long Lane, London EC1A 9PN

www.scm-canterburypress.co.uk



British Library Cataloguing in Publication data

A catalogue record for this book is available
from the British Library

ISBN 978-1-85311-897-5

Typeset by Regent Typesetting, London
Printed in the UK by
CPI William Clowes Beccles NR34 7TL

This book is dedicated to the memory of Andrew Adano and William Waqo, evangelists, friends and successive assistant bishops of Marsabit, in the north of Kenya. They died ten years apart, in Marsabit: Andrew in a helicopter accident in 1996, and William in a plane crash in 2006.

The royalties of this book are given to the Adano Fund of the Church Mission Society. This was set up in June 1999 for the charity walk, organized by the author, in memory of Andrew, 'Oxford to Cambridge with a Camel', in which William took part. The fund provides help for schools for the children of camel-based nomads, founded by Andrew, in the semi-arid area around Marsabit (www.cms-uk.org/adano).

# Contents

## The Prayer Stool

I leave aside my shoes, my ambitions;
    undo my watch, my timetable;
    take off my glasses, my views;
    unclip my pen, my work;
    put down my keys, my security;
    to be alone with you,
        the only true God.
After being with you,
    I take up my shoes to walk in your ways;
    strap on my watch to live in your time;
    put on my glasses to look at your world;
    clip on my pen to write up your thoughts;
    pick up my keys to open your doors.

Graham Kings, 1986

# Foreword

## by the Bishop of Durham, Dr N. T. Wright

Students at one theological college were sent off to a betting shop and told to place a bet. Most of these clergy-in-training had never done such a thing before, and were ill at ease: is everyone looking at me? What am I supposed to do? Will I let it out that I haven't a clue what's going on?

The point, of course, was that that's how many people feel today when they go into a church. In the same way, many who find themselves, to their own surprise, coming to believe that Jesus of Nazareth is the living embodiment of the loving God who made the world, feel unsure of their new surroundings. How does it all work? Yes, I may have discovered God calling me by name; I may have realized that Jesus died and rose again *for me*; but what happens now? Will I ever feel at home with all this new language, with people doing and saying odd things and assuming everybody knows what it's all about?

This book is written for people like that – and many more besides, since we all need an occasional 'refresher course'. Graham Kings is the vicar of one of London's liveliest churches and theological secretary of Fulcrum. A theologian, mystic, poet and entrepreneur, he invites us to come on a journey through countryside familiar to most experienced Christians but often bewildering to newcomers. He is an encouraging and entertaining guide.

The journey in question is the Christian year – Advent, Christmas, Epiphany, Lent, Good Friday, Easter, Pentecost, Trinity. From very early on, Christians have not just *told* the great story of the plan of God to save and renew the world. They have also *lived* this story, following the biblical narrative through the year and so, like a family marking birthdays and other anniversaries, reminding themselves constantly who they are and why. God's preparation of his people; his coming in the person of his Son; Jesus' life, death and resurrection; the sending of the Spirit – these are not odd, detached beliefs, but tell a great story, a play in which we are all invited to become actors in our own right.

Graham Kings brings all this to life briefly and vividly. He introduces some fresh and perhaps controversial ideas; he would be the last person to say that everyone should agree with everything he says! But he not only explains the map of the Christian journey and encourages us all to keep travelling; he allows the book to embody one of its own great themes, that of new creation. Through shrewd use of art, displaying and discussing paintings and sculptures with which he has himself been involved, he turns this book into a multi-media experience. And, through some of his own poems, he not only illustrates his themes but encourages us all, through meditation and contemplation, to discover the truth that, as St Paul says, 'we are God's work of art, God's poem' (Ephesians 2.10). This book will open the mind to fresh truth while opening the imagination to glimpses of glory.

†THOMAS DUNELM

The Rt Revd N. T. Wright, DD
Bishop of Durham

# Preface

Imagine the year ahead of you. What comes to mind? When does that year begin? Whose year is it? How do you make God smile? You tell him your plans . . .

God sees further and wider than you see, knows you better than you know yourself, and loves you more than you have ever been loved.

The year ahead for you belongs to God. It is his and he gives it to you, to your family and friends, to your community and to the world. Quite a year, then. Not worth cramping its imagining and not worth rushing either. A spiritual writer of great wisdom once wrote, 'Hurry is actually a form of violence exercised upon God's time in order to make it "my time"' (Donald Nicholl, *Holiness*). The seasonal rhythm of the year, which has been kept for centuries by the Church across the world, may have something to offer you. How about imagining your year fitting in with the Church's year?

Rhythm is not only the longest English word without a vowel – though admittedly 'y' acts as a sort of vowel – but is also basic to our enjoyment in life. We breathe, walk and swim rhythmically, usually without noticing it. We appreciate music, poetry and drama. We become more balanced in our quality of life when rhythms develop naturally. In this book, we shall be looking together at the rhythm, balance and journey of the Church's year. Each chapter has a focus on a particular season: Advent, Christmas, Epiphany, Lent, Good Friday, Easter, Pentecost and Trinity. Each chapter also has a dynamic participle (an '-ing' word) which relates to the season of the year: beginning, being, sharing, suffering, dying, rising, living and identifying.

Questions are provocative and can be central to learning. Children abound with them and sadly, too often, we leave them behind as we degenerate into adulthood. Each chapter has a question and my responses to them provide signs for your journey – works of art, poems and comments on some passages of Scripture. You will still have lots of questions by the end of the book and it would be good to interact with these together through the book's website www.signsandseasons.co.uk.

Art is evocative and can be moving. I've chosen eight works with which I have been involved, and which have moved me towards God – one from Indonesia, three from England, two from a Bulgarian artist, one from Kenya, and one from India. I've also interwoven with these works poems that I've written at different times in Kenya, Cambridge and London. Do be patient with me and, if these particular poems don't light up for you, then just turn over the page – or, better still, pause a bit, and write some poetry yourself. Again, these poems could be shared on the website.

In Scripture, God speaks to us through his reliable ancient words, which come alive across the centuries in surprising ways. We need to understand their meaning in their original contexts and interpret their significance faithfully and imaginatively for today. I wrote much of this in the new British Library, not far from our church in Islington, while there was an amazing exhibition of the world's greatest collection of Jewish, Christian and Muslim holy books, called 'Sacred'. It was very popular. Two precious texts in particular struck me. Codex Sinaiticus is the earliest complete New Testament from fourth-century Egypt or Palestine, and the Lindisfarne Gospels is the luminous legacy of an artist monk in Northumbria in the early eighth century.

Imagining the journey of a year can be exhilarating and risky. As a family, we lived in the foothills of Mount Kenya for seven years and I walked up Mount Kenya twice. On one occasion we got to the top of Point Lenana, the third highest peak, about 16,000 feet, and the highest that can be reached without climbing equipment. The view showed the curvature of the Earth and Mount Kilimanjaro in the distance. The second time, we had to come down, having walked to 9,600 feet, because some of our group had altitude sickness. Our Kenyan guides were indispensable for the journey. They gave signs, directions and assistance in carrying, and also provided wisdom about timing and advice on turning back when necessary.

A journey of faith can begin at any time, and the beginning can be a process over a period of time – for example, an Alpha course, which is a very popular introduction to Christianity over several weeks – or a particular point of focus. It often turns out that even those people who have a definable moment of commitment ultimately discover many significant movements and people in the background leading up to this moment. Beginnings can be topsy-turvy. My own life was turned upside down as a student in January 1974. In one week, as a law student at Oxford, my faith in Jesus Christ came alive, on the Sunday; I met my future wife on the Wednesday; and I joined a prayer group for God's mission in the world on the Friday.

If you have recently begun a journey of faith – either through a long process or one focal point – then this book is designed for you as a guide as you imagine your year ahead and seek further understanding for your faith. Belief is vocative and usually vocational, in that it is addressed to God, rather than to ourselves, and leads into God calling us to change and to serve. This may seem scary at this stage, but – in the words of both *The Hitchhikers Guide to the Galaxy* and *Dad's Army* – don't panic.

Some of the following art, poems and thoughts I shared at a Methodist conference on world mission in 2006, and a year later at the Chelmsford Diocesan retreat house at Pleshey, with those on retreat, preparing for ordination to the priesthood. Over many years, Pleshey was the Anglican base of Evelyn Underhill, the imaginative spiritual writer. In her book *The Light of Christ* (London, 1944) she commented on the rhythm of life:

> We get notions sometimes that we ought to spring up quickly like seed on stony ground, we ought to show some startling sign of spiritual growth. But perhaps we are only asked to go on quietly, to be a child, a nice stocky seedling, not shooting up in a hurry, but making root, being docile to the great slow rhythm of life. When you don't see any startling marks of your own religious condition or your usefulness to God, think of the baby in the stable and the little

> boy in the streets of Nazareth. The very life there which was to change the whole history of the human race. There was not much to show for it. But there is entire continuity between the stable and the Easter garden and the thread that unites them is the will of God. The childlike simple prayer of Nazareth was the right preparation for the awful privilege of the cross. Just so the light of the Spirit is to unfold gently and steadily within us, till at last our final stature, all God designed for us, is attained.

So I hope that you will join me on this journey, as we ponder signs and seasons, and that it may turn out for you to be exhilarating, balanced, provocative, evocative, illuminating and patient.

Graham Kings
Islington, London
Easter 2008

# Beginning

## ADVENT

### Where do we come from and where are we going to?

The questions 'where do we come from?' and 'where are we going to?' are foundational to our faith. They remind me of early evening walks on the red soil of the foothills of Mount Kenya. Friends would greet me with the Kikuyu phrase, 'wa thii ko?' ('where are you going?') and 'uma ko?' (where are you from?').

It may seem strange, but beginnings and endings are closely linked. The Christian Year begins with Advent, four Sundays before Christmas Day. The background meaning of the word 'Advent' is 'coming' or, to be more personal, 'the one who is coming'. The season is full of waiting expectancy. Traditionally the biblical readings of the first weeks focus on the end of the world, and these are followed by the preparations for the birth of Jesus. So, Advent looks forward to both the dramatic summing up of history, when everything is wrapped up and recreated, and also towards the subtle and subversive arrival of a baby, whose life is in fact the secret centre of the universe.

We shall be adjusting that tradition a little, by first looking back to creation, 'where do we come from?' before moving on to consider 'where are we going to?' With increased Christian concern for our planet and its delicate ecological balance, there have been discussions concerning where in the Christian Year there should be a focus on creation. Since it involves beginnings and – if we don't act on these issues seriously – 'endings', then perhaps Advent may be advocated?

Take a long look at the Indonesian batik, with its burst of explosive energy. I bought it a few years ago, at Camden Lock Market in London, for my wife, Alison. The room at home where she works matches the blues and whites and it hangs there now. Most people in Indonesia are Muslims – but this particular batik artist, I discovered from the owner of the shop, is a Christian. His name is Aryo Pratyoto Kuswadji (better known as Aprat), and he works in Yogyakarta, Central Java.

Indonesian batik, Aryo Pratyoto Kuswadji.
(See colour section)

His work speaks to me of an amazing explosion of creation out of nothingness, a short, sudden and intense period of activity resulting in a phenomenal pattern. It seems to me to resonate with the cosmological concept of the original Big Bang of the universe. The blue sphere in the centre reminds me of photos of our planet from space. The swirl of the white below it can turn it into a model of the current World Cup trophy. (Well, from the sublime to the ridiculous maybe.)

John Humphrys, the veteran terrier-like presenter and interviewer of BBC Radio 4's *Today* programme, recently published an intriguingly sympathetic book entitled *In God We Doubt* based on a series of interviews he presented on Radio 4 called 'In Search of God'. In his book, Humphrys admits he is still searching. He begins with recalling how as a young boy in Wales he came up with some key questions such as, 'what is the universe in?' – in other words, 'what is *beyond* the universe?'

A quick answer to the questions we began with may well be 'we come from God and we are going to God'. However, a long answer perhaps may be found in Psalm 104, right in the middle of the Bible. The book of Psalms, it is worth remembering, was Jesus' own 'prayer book'. You may have expected me to begin with the book of Genesis – which actually means 'Beginning' – but it is more fun to begin in the middle, because from there we can look back and look forward.

Psalm 104 begins and ends with an invitation to worship, and an expression of praise, 'Bless the Lord, O my soul! O Lord my God, you are very great.' In our own lives, being caught up in the wonder of creation naturally leads many of us into worship. The whole Psalm describes the cycle of the Palestinian agricultural year and includes God's initial creation and his continuing, sustaining power. It has similarities both to Genesis chapter 1 and to the spectacular poem of creation in Job chapters 38 and 39, as well as some echoes of Egyptian writings.

Sky, clouds, wind, earth, waters, mountains and valleys are created in verses 2–9 in Psalm 104. God provides for springs, animals and birds in verses 10–13 and then, in verses 13 and 15, we reach human beings. There are plants to cultivate, wine to gladden hearts, and oil to make faces to shine and work for their labour (v. 23). The list tumbles on into specifics with cedars, storks, goats, badgers, moon and sun, lions. At verse 24 there is a pause for breath – 'O Lord, how manifold are your works! In wisdom you have make them all' – before launching off again with the fish, ships and sea monsters. In verse 26 in Psalm 104, the poet strikes while the irony is hot. God forms the most huge, powerful sea monster ever, Leviathan (just see his scary description in Job chapter 41), whose purpose is delightfully circumscribed as 'to sport in the sea'. Leviathan, as a symbol of ultimate power, is cut down to size, as God's plaything.

All God's creatures look to him for their food in due season (v. 27), and they rely on him completely for life or death (vv. 28–30). God's breath and his Spirit are the same word in Hebrew, and verse 30 links in the importance of God's Spirit in the creative process, which may be compared with the 'wind from God' or 'Spirit of God' brooding over the waters of creation in Genesis chapter 1. Verse 31, 'may the Lord rejoice in his works', echoes the regular, rhythmic refrain of Genesis chapter 1: 'And the Lord saw that it was good.'

Earthquakes and volcanoes are mentioned in a late flourish, before the assurance of continuing praise. The desire for sinners and the wicked to be consumed may appear to be discordant just before the final expression of praise, but many modern ecological campaigners speak vociferously against those who destroy God's creation. The Psalms have all the range of emotions.

When looking at a passage from Scripture, it is important to consider what sort of literature it is. Psalm 104 is both poetry and one of the great Psalms of wisdom. It is usually classified as a key example of 'wisdom literature' in the Bible, which concerns practical suggestions for godly living and sometimes has affinities with other literature in the Ancient Near East. The Psalm has echoes of a famous Egyptian hymn to the sun (fourteenth century BC) composed by the Pharaoh Akhenaten. He was way ahead of his time in stressing the importance of belief in only one God and in worshipping not the sun, but its maker. Sadly, his amazing leap of insight died with him and Egyptian religion continued on with beliefs in many gods.

God's revelation of himself in the Bible was not in a hermetically sealed bubble, nor via dictation. It was set in the context of many nations and cultures in the Ancient Near East. There are echoes of other stories, poems and myths, but these are transformed under the inspiration of God's Holy Spirit, for the education of his people.

It is interesting to compare this Psalm with a modern ecological litany from Kenya.

## Litany for the Preservation of the Environment

May the shaved hills be reforested,
**And turn flourishingly green again.**

May the forests grow denser and greener,
**May the encroachment of the deserts be averted.**

May the rivers stay in their courses,
**And be safeguarded against pollution.**

May the fields yield a hundred fold,
**And people be well fed;**

May the herds and the flocks ever find green pasture and cooling streams;
**May our seas, oceans and lakes teem with aquatic life;**

May all wildlife be protected;
**May it be safeguarded against poaching and fire catastrophes;**

May water gush forth in the deserts and springs in the wastelands.
**May creation harmony be furthered and humanity be truly good stewards as was decreed in the garden of Eden.**

Glory to the Father, Son and Holy Spirit,
**As it was in the beginning, is now and ever shall be. Amen.**

Anglican Church of Kenya, *Our Modern Services* (pp. 227–28)

People in the nations surrounding the Jews often worshipped parts of 'nature' as 'divine'. Psalm 104, though, is very different. When nature is emptied of so-called 'divinity' it is set free to express and symbolize God himself or God's word (as in Psalm 19).

So, let's now move back to the beginning of the Bible, to Genesis chapter 1. This is another poetic-style presentation of creation. Sadly, it sometimes becomes an arguing ground between 'six-day creationists' – that is, those who insist on taking it absolutely literally – and 'secular evolutionists' – those who write God out of any involvement in creation. There is a third, more appropriate, position it seems to me, taken by 'theistic evolutionists'. We treat God's word in this chapter seriously, but not literally, and believe that God created through the process of evolution.

To 'six-day creationists', my response has been to point out that to force the theological heights of Genesis chapter 1 into the wrong categories of scientific fact and detailed history leads to unimagined contradictions with the university disciplines of theology, geology, biology, archaeology and anthropology. God's universe is clearly and evidently more ancient than a few thousand years, and his creation of human beings through an evolutionary process does not detract from his glory. Genesis chapter 1 primarily answers the questions 'who and why?' rather than 'how and when?' It was God who created – the universe did not just 'happen' – and he created it for his delight and enjoyment.

In discussions with people who interpret this chapter literally, I have sometimes read with them the second story of creation – in Genesis chapter 2. This has a different shape, style, vocabulary and name for God (Lord God), as well as a different order of events in which he creates. Have a look at it. In Genesis chapter 2 man is made first (v. 7), then plants (vv. 8–9), then animals (vv. 19–20) and finally woman (vv. 21–22). This contradicts the order in Genesis chapter 1, where plants are made first (vv. 11–13), then fish, birds and animals (vv. 20–25), and finally human beings, both men and women at the same time (vv. 26–27). These orders are not only different, but also contradictory. People who believe in the literal interpretation of Genesis also usually stress that God does not contradict himself in his Word. If these two stories of creation, in their literal interpretation, do indeed contradict themselves concerning the order of events, then surely God does not want us to take them literally? If the 'editor' of the two stories from different authors, inspired by the Holy Spirit, was relaxed about putting them together, then we should read and ponder both of them imaginatively and theologically.

Where are we going to? Well, to God. All of us, one day, will meet him. From my reading and pondering of the Scriptures, I believe that there will be recognition and re-creation, but also judgement and de-creation. Some assume – and presume – that everyone will live with God eternally. He forgives, that is his job, isn't it? Others insist on the literal and perpetual destruction of hell-fire for all those who don't openly respond to the good news of Christ. I disagree with both these extremes.

The difficulty of the first assumption is Jesus' own warnings that not all will enter into the kingdom of God. If the most loving person who ever existed also gave such serious warnings, then we should not presume to disagree. The danger of the second insistence is that such eternal torture does not match the character of God, which we see fully revealed in Jesus Christ.

In this, I was helped by thinking over the amazing, ultimate purpose of God, 'a plan for the fullness of time', which Paul mentions in Ephesians 1.10 is 'to gather up all things in Christ, things in heaven and things on earth'. How did that fit with the warnings of Jesus in the Gospels and the fact that love does not involve using force against someone's will? How could all things be gathered up in Christ, when some, who were clearly not in Christ and really did not want to respond to God, would be judged for eternity?

I was also assisted by meditating on the meaning of the word 'eternal' in the phrase 'eternal destruction'. Did it refer to the eternal *acts* of destroying (that is, they would continue for ever), or did it refer to the eternal *effect* of destruction (that is, what was destroyed would never be re-created)?

From these considerations, I believe that there will, tragically, still be some who reject the generous offer of the free love of God in Jesus Christ. On the last day when they meet God 'face to face', he will not force them to change their decision about him – for love does not force. He will underline their decision and they will be de-created back into the nothingness out of which creation originally came. In their case, it will be 'from nothing, to nothing'. So the 'de-creation into nothingness' would be the meaning of the phrase 'eternal destruction'. Then, all creation – everyone and everything in heaven and earth that would be left – would indeed be in Christ and be summed up in him.

The inner meaning of the season of Advent is expressed beautifully in the particular Anglican prayer, traditionally called a 'collect' because of its 'gathering' nature, for the first Sunday in Advent:

Almighty God,
give us grace to cast away the works of darkness
and to put on the armour of light,
now in the time of this mortal life,
in which your Son Jesus Christ came to us in great humility,
that on the last day,
when he shall come again in his glorious majesty
  to judge the living and the dead,
we may rise to the life immortal;
through him who is alive and reigns with you,
in the unity of the Holy Spirit,
one God, now and for ever.

The Archbishops' Council, *Common Worship: Services and Prayers for the Church of England* (p. 376)

The epistle set to be read at Holy Communion for the first Sunday in Advent is Romans 13.11–14, where Paul gives a warning call: 'It is now the moment for you to wake from sleep.' It was this passage that had a huge turning effect on the life of St Augustine (AD 354–430). He was the great father of Western theology and was Bishop of Hippo (in what is now Algeria). His autobiography up to his conversion, *Confessions*, was written as a prayer – autobiography addressed to God. Augustine was a professor of rhetoric in Milan, and for 14 years had lived with his partner. In Book VIII he described his agony of decision, while walking in a garden, concerning conversion and baptism. The singing of a child nearby prompted him to take up the Scriptures and read. The book was open at Romans 13.11–14.

I wrote the following poem during a conference at Yale University. It was inspired by the first chapter of a book, *Divine Discourse* (CUP, 1995), by Nicholas Wolterstorff, the Yale philosopher and theologian. The chapter reflects on the story of Augustine in the garden.

## Turning Point

> Give me chastity and continence, but not yet.

Confessions VIII, 7

> Put on the Lord Jesus Christ, and make no provision for the flesh, to gratify its desires.

Romans 13.14

Stalking in the garden in the heat of the moment,
Reflecting on complexity of voluntary movement,
Slunk in listless and leaden despair,
Tangled, contorted and tearing his hair,
Rapping his head and wrapping his knees,
Rabidly ravaging under the trees,
Wanting to wait and waiting to want,
Weighing the longing of laying and font,
Augustine hears the Word of the Lord
Drifting, insisting the voice of a child:
'Tolle, lege: take it and read.
Tolle, lege: take it and read.'
Vocative discourse spoken by God,
Evocative sing-song challenge of a child.

Turning and turning he opens to read
The Word of the Lord in the words of St Paul:
'Lust and debauchery, revelry, rivalry,
Now is the time to wake from your sleep.'
Eloquent professor professes his call.

Now, no procrastination, delay;
Later is now, tomorrow today.

# Being

# CHRISTMAS

## How is God involved in his world?

If God created the universe and it reflects his glory, but nature itself is not 'divine' nor an extension of his divinity, then how is he involved in his world? And this really is his world. Some Christians give the impression that only the Church belongs to God and the world has gone to ruin, and they have to take God into the world. But God is not a small, partial, portable god – he is God of the whole world, not just a segment of it. If he is involved, then he calls us to be involved too.

God's focal point of entry into his own world we celebrate in the season of Christmas. Now don't worry about the probability that in the mid-fourth century the date of 25 December was chosen to counteract the midwinter Roman pagan festival of the Sun. No one actually knows the real date of the nativity, but a date was needed for the rhythm of the year, and the reinterpretation of a well-known festival was a point worth making. Dates develop by regular use into tradition, and tradition, as G. K. Chesterton memorably observed, is the 'democracy of the dead'.

God takes his material world seriously, so much so that he became part of it, embodied and embedded. I love the irony of Archbishop

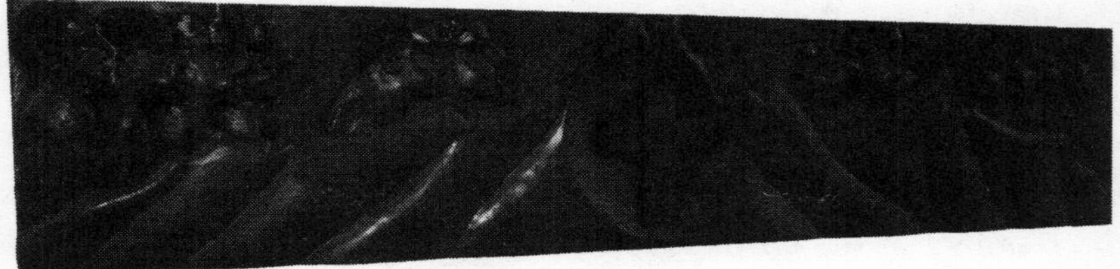

'Facing Mount Kenya', Benson Ndaka. (See colour section)

William Temple's profound remark: 'Christianity is the most materialistic of all religions'. This is because of our doctrines of creation and incarnation. In the first, God is distinct from his creation; in the second, in Christ, he became part of it.

Have a long look at the photo of the carving, 'Facing Mount Kenya' by Benson Ndaka. I met Benson in 1989 when I was on retreat at a Benedictine monastery at Tigoni, just north-west of Nairobi. He was a 'carver in residence', working in a basement workshop, and had carved the various wonderful doors of the monastery. The Abbot kindly gave permission for Benson to be commissioned to carve the mahogany doors of our new library at St Andrew's College, Kabare, near Mount Kenya. In traditional Kikuyu religion, people would face Mount Kenya to pray, and be buried pointing towards the mountain.

This particular carving hangs in the entrance hall of the library and reflects the shape of the twin peaks of the mountain top, viewed from Kabare. The mountain represents God the Father, and the cross embedded at the heart of the mountain, God the Son. The Holy Spirit is echoed in the rivers flowing down the mountain and the Church is summed up in the apostles, in Kenyan style, at the top. So various strands of theology resonate and interweave in one carving.

The traditional Christmas Day Gospel reading is John 1.1–14. Have a look at it and ponder its meaning and significance. It is not usually seen as a daring attempt at 'cross-cultural communication', but that is what it is, by both God and the author. When the Word became flesh, God crossed the widest cultural gap in the universe. He plumbed the depths and used body language to communicate. In Jesus, the Ultimate became intimate. As John tried to interpret the good news to both Jews and Greeks he chose a metaphor that was full of meaning for both – the Word. In the Hebrew Scriptures God said 'Let there be light' (Genesis 1) and the heavens were made by the word of the Lord (Psalm 33). In popular Greek philosophical thought, the Word (*Logos*) was the meaning of the universe, the reason, the mind, the first principle behind everything. The author used and infused these ideas with his own focus – the Word is personal and, astonishingly, became flesh. In many ways this is a crude term which implied something low and frail. Thus God shows us that 'matter' does in fact matter.

Here are two poems based on this passage. The first, written for a carol service, takes up this theme.

## Matter of Great Moment

For God, matter matters:
For the Word became flesh.

In the beginning was the Meaning,
And the Meaning became matter,
And the matter became moment,
And the moment became movement,
And the Meaning moved us.

For God, matter matters:
For the Word became flesh.

The theme is important in understanding God's mission and following in his wake – and, as we shall see in Chapter 6, it also relates to the doctrine of resurrection. Some Christians imply that the body, or society, being things that last only a short time, are not eternally significant for God and so should not be part of our mission. But in this passage, the emphasis is evident on the body, 'became flesh', and on society, 'and lived among us' – literally 'put up his tent among us'. The gospel as a whole shows us that God has honoured our human bodies and society by becoming fully part of our humanity and social condition.

While at Kabare, I vividly remember questions from students about the doctrine of Christ – that Jesus was fully divine yet fully human. He was not half and half, and not an 'in-between figure' – he was fully both and fully integrated. I developed the metaphor of 'the song' to illustrate this. A song is made up of words (divinity) and music (humanity) and, when sung, these two interweave together inextricably. This emerged into a poem:

**The Gospel of the Song**

In the beginning were the Words,
 and the Words were the Poet's,
 and they were part of Him:
 lively and brilliant.

And the Words became music,
 and were sung,
 full of beauty and freedom.

We have heard the Song,
 and been utterly moved,
 again and again.

We had read poetry before,
 but beauty and freedom
 came through this Song.

No-one has ever seen the Poet:
 this one Song, which is in His heart,
 has shown Him to us.

God is involved in his world through this man, who was much more than just a man. Sometimes it is easier to approach the question of who Jesus was – and is – through his humanity. Martin Luther, the German monk and theologian who sparked off the Reformation in the sixteenth century, once suggested: 'Take hold of Jesus as a man and you will discover that he is God.'

Perhaps it may be better to take hold of him first as a child? Have a look at the lovely story of Jesus at the age of 12 in Luke 2.41–52, and especially at the last verse: 'Jesus grew in wisdom and stature, in favour with God and people'. This was a favourite verse of David Gitari, the Bishop of Mount Kenya East. Jesus actually *grew* in wisdom. Has it dawned on you that he did not know everything, and that what he did know did not come to him all at once, ready packaged? He never knew during his 30 years or so, for example, about helicopters and computers. He was fully a first-century Palestinian Jewish man. Yet his insights from God were extraordinary and developed early, as can be seen in this passage, with his question and answer session in the Temple. In his ministry, he was perceptive in reading the political and spiritual signs of the times, and prophetic in denouncing the hypocrisy of religious leaders and the general direction of Israel, which was heading towards disaster and destruction.

From his mother Mary, Jesus would have learnt how to speak (his mother-tongue was Aramaic) and how to eat and drink and move. I was struck by this concept while watching the opening of Act Two in *The Mysteries*, the spectacular South African update of the medieval Chester mystery plays. It played to packed houses at the Wilton Music Hall in the East End of London, and one Sunday morning in 2002 the cast performed part of it at a guest service in St Mary's Church. The vibrancy and energy of the story and portrayals by the multi-racial actors were extraordinary. The second act opened with Mary teaching Jesus to do a rhythmic 'hand-slap' dance, which involved hands slapping knees, thighs and feet. At first, he could not follow her actions – and this produced much laughter in Mary and the audience – but then he did, and used the dance effectively to call his disciples. Hauntingly, the disciples used it again as a greeting when they saw Jesus in the Upper Room after the resurrection.

As well as growing in wisdom (his mind), Jesus also increased in stature (his body), in favour with God (his spirit) and in favour with people (his community). So we have before us here, in Luke chapter 2, an intriguing doctrine of human beings – 'mind, body and spirit in community'. Jesus not only showed us who God really is, but he also showed us who we are meant to be – mature human beings. We are not just a 'mind', nor a 'mind in a body', nor even 'mind, body and spirit in isolation from other people', but 'mind, body and spirit in community'. Balanced growth in all four areas, following the example of Christ, leads to wholeness and to authentic worship, which itself should include all four aspects of our humanity.

So if the focus of God's involvement in his world is through the incarnation – the Word becoming flesh – how else is he involved? Part of the answer is by his Holy Spirit. The Spirit was at work in creation, in the poetic image of 'brooding over the waters' in the beginning. This continued through millions of years of evolution, as the Spirit drew nature upwards towards the full stature of humanity. We should be astounded at the personal, attractive power of God, summoning his own creation onwards and upwards.

The influence of the Spirit is evident throughout Luke's first chapters leading up to the story we have just considered. There seems to have been almost a flood of the Spirit after a long drought. John the Baptist was filled with the Spirit while he grew in the womb (Luke 1.15). His mother, Elizabeth, and father, Zechariah, burst into response and song inspired by the Spirit (Luke 1.41–45 and 68–79). Jesus' mother, Mary, unmarried and a virgin, was overshadowed by the Spirit and rejoiced in song (Luke 1.30–35 and 46–55). The Spirit 'rested' on Simeon, the old man in the Temple, 'revealed' a promise to him, and 'guided' him to meet, bless and prophesy over the infant Jesus. As we shall see in Chapter 7, Luke continues to develop the theme of the Holy Spirit throughout his Gospel and his Acts of the Apostles.

Another aspect of God's involvement in his world comes out in Luke's carefully detailed description of the dating and political context of Jesus' birth, under the yoke of Imperial Rome (Luke 2.1–2 and 3.1–2). God was, and is, shaping the direction of history and the nations – not in a mechanical, puppet-master way, but by weaving his ways into his world and drawing it towards his purposes. International politics in the Ancient Near East, in the Roman Empire and today, are not outside of his sphere of influence. However, he is not a totalitarian God, who dictates every event throughout the whole of history. People and politicians have their own responsible choices and, sadly, many events happen that are contrary to God's desires – just one example being the passing of the apartheid laws of South Africa. He works within the awfulness of oppressive regimes (of the 'right' and of the 'left') to bring about liberation. Sometimes this is through his people who know him and sometimes it is through those who don't. God is not limited in scope or people, and nor is he constricted into a box called the 'spiritual realm'.

There is a wonderful Filipino proverb, 'God writes straight with crooked lines', which illustrates this well. It was a very popular saying at the time of the bloodless revolution in June 1986 which toppled the dictator of the Philippines, President Marcos. Over two days, two million people came on to the streets of Manila and at times it was not clear how the army would react. Amazingly, nuns placed flowers in the gun barrels of tanks, and many lay down in front of their tracks. The leader of the Roman Catholic Church in the Philippines spoke on the radio and encouraged people to demonstrate peacefully. His name was Cardinal Sin, and this led to many puns. Some of these puns were friendly, such as his words of welcome to visitors when they arrived at his home – 'welcome to the house of Sin'. Others were threatening, such as Marcos's threat that he would show the people that he was a 'mortal Sin'.

In June 1989, I was in Manila for a conference on mission and bought a photojournalism book of the events of 1986 from the former presidential palace, which had been turned into a museum. On the Sunday, I worshipped in a charismatic Catholic church and was asked to bring greetings from England. I mentioned the book and asked if any of the congregation had been on the streets in those momentous days, three years earlier. About three-quarters of them put up their hands and, at the end of the service, they signed the inside cover of the book.

So we have seen that God's involvement in his world is both from 'without' and from 'within'. His eternal Word comes from 'outside'

Indonesian batik,
Aryo Pratyoto Kuswadji.
Advent, page 2

'Facing Mount Kenya', Benson Ndaka. Christmas, page 11

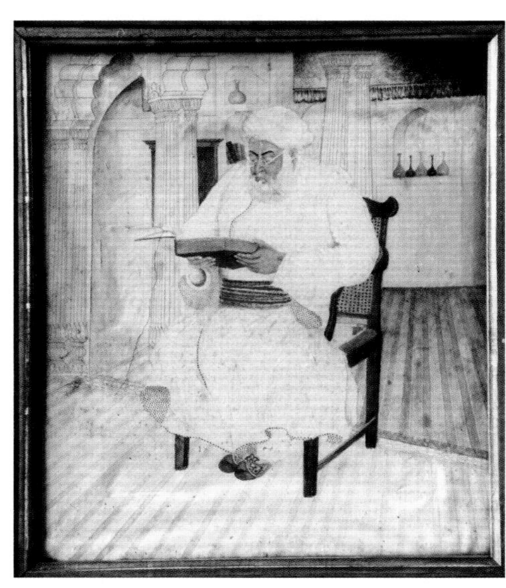

'The Revd Abdul Masseeh,
Henry Martyn's one convert',
painter unknown.
Epiphany, page 19

'Christ Blessing the Children', Jonathan Clarke. Lent, page 30

'The Eighth Hour', Jonathan Clarke. Good Friday, page 38

'Rabbouni', Silvia Dimitrova. Easter, page 46

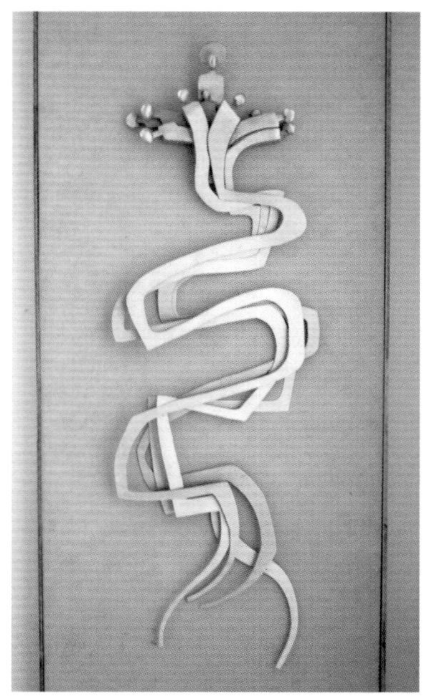

'Way of Life',
Jonathan Clarke.
Pentecost, page 54

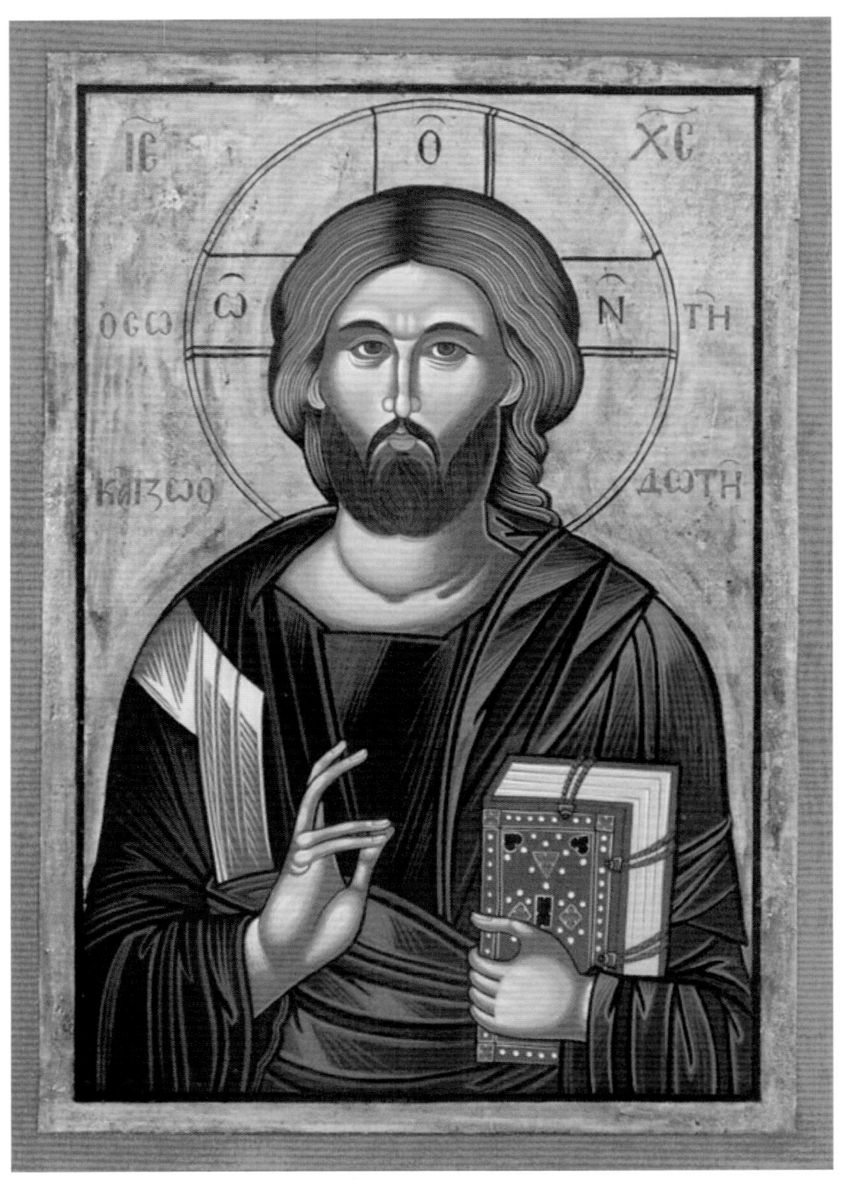


'Jesus Christ, Saviour and Giver of Life', Silvia Dimitrova. Trinity, page 62

creation, bringing it into being at the beginning and 'irrupting' into it at the centre – at the very first Christmas. His eternal Spirit works patiently deep 'within' creation and history, and also 'erupts' at key moments – like molten lava.

We are called to discern and trace what is going on in the events that are taking place. God's providence has always raised awkward questions and we finish this chapter with a wry story about Frederick Temple. While he was Archbishop of Canterbury, he was approached by a woman who had a question to ask him. Her aunt had been due to board a ship. At the last moment, she missed the ship which sank during its voyage. Did the Archbishop think that was a case of providential interference? He replied, 'Can't tell. Didn't know your aunt.'

# Sharing

## EPIPHANY

### What do we have to share with others?

The season of Epiphany, which means literally 'manifestation', begins on 6 January with the celebration of the wise men arriving in Bethlehem to give gifts to the infant Christ (Matthew 2.1–12). They come from the East and are not Jewish. Epiphany ends on 2 February with the presentation of Christ at the Temple by his parents (Luke 2.21–38). There, an elderly man named Simeon prophesies that Christ will be a light for revelation to the Gentiles – the non-Jews – and glory for God's people, Israel. So Epiphany is a season for sharing the good news with all people. This revelation of the good news of Christ to people of other faiths, and their coming to him, has been echoed throughout the ages.

In 1993, the recently appointed Principal of Ridley Hall theological college in Cambridge, Graham Cray, discovered a painting in a cupboard and immediately shared the good news of it with me. There was no written clue on the front of the painting, but on turning it over the following words could be seen in ink: 'The Revd Abdul Masseeh. Henry Martyn's one convert – ordained by Bishop Heber. Revd G. E. Corrie, Jesus Coll: Cambridge. Luggage Train.' I was the Henry

Martyn Lecturer in mission studies in Ridley and the other theological colleges in Cambridge, so questions came thick and fast to me.

Who was the seated Indian so serene and calm? What was he reading, with concentrated meditation, that was so evidently precious? What were the books and bottles in the background? Why was he celebrated with such a commissioned portrait? Who was this man who spans the centuries, and today speaks to us in his silence and draws us into studying what he himself was reading?

The painting is a watercolour and bodycolour over graphite on medium weight, wove paper. Its painter, date, provenance, history and acquisition by Ridley Hall are all mysteries, but the people mentioned are fascinating. Abdul Masih – the more usual spelling of his name – (1776–1827) was a Muslim who came to faith in Christ through the preaching of Henry Martyn (1781–1812), a chaplain of the East India Company, pioneer missionary scholar and Bible translator. Masih became a medical missionary and evangelist among his own people, supported by the Church Missionary Society (CMS), and in 1825 became the second Indian ordained Anglican clergyman. George Corrie (1793–1885) was a Fellow, and later Master, of Jesus College, Cambridge, and his connection with India was through his brother, Daniel Corrie (1777–1837). The latter was Martyn's great friend, Masih's mentor and, as Archdeacon of Calcutta, was present at Masih's ordination. Reginald Heber (1783–1826) was the Bishop of Calcutta. It seems

'The Revd Abdul Masseeh, Henry Martyn's one convert', painter unknown. (See colour section)

very likely to me that Corrie was the person who commissioned this painting, as an ordination portrait, and that after his death it was sent to his brother George in Cambridge.

Heber's fine description of Masih, in his personal journal for 12 January 1825, captures the character we see in this portrait: 'His long eastern dress, his long grey beard, and his calm resigned countenance give him already the air of an Apostle.' The *Missionary Papers* of CMS in 1831 excelled itself with a delicate description, which may have some backing from the painting: 'latterly, an unnatural tendency to corpulency rendered long journeys irksome'.

Masih's original name was Sheik Salih. He was born in Delhi about the year 1776, and became a zealous Muslim. When working for an officer in the East India Company he even induced a Hindu servant to become a Muslim. In 1810 he was at Cawnpore, in northern India, and heard Henry Martyn preach to the poor who assembled at his door on Sunday afternoons to receive alms. Salih, in his own words, went 'to see the sport'. He was struck by Martyn's exposition of the Ten Commandments and wanted to hear more. In the end he was engaged to work with Martyn's assistant.

The CMS *Missionary Papers* documented his conversion in 1810:

> When Mr Martyn had finished his Translation of the New Testament into Hindoostanee, the book was given to Sheik Salih to bind. This he considered as a fine opportunity; nor did he let it slip. On reading the Word of God, he discovered his state, and perceived therein a true description of his own heart. He soon decided in favour of the Christian Religion.

So the book held so reverently by Masih in the painting is significant, and it is probably an edition of Henry Martyn's Hindustani New Testament. It forms the ultimate focus of both him and of the portrait. He is not looking out at us, but down at the Scriptures that convicted him, translated by the man who convinced him. Our eyes are also drawn to that point, as we perceive ourselves to be witnesses of the biblical devotion of one bound to Christ, and so ultimately Christ-bound, by his binding of the Scriptures. He seems to have taken to heart the words of the Anglican collect for 'Bible Sunday' – to 'read, mark, learn and inwardly digest' the Holy Scriptures.

When we were living in Kenya, we sometimes spent holidays at the coast. The following poem was written in 1988 after I visited a mosque in Mombasa.

## Is Jesus the Son of Allah?

Kneeling alone on the soft carpet
of a Mombasa mosque,
chandeliers above, galleries around,
stereo system stacked high in the corner,
the quiet question came to me –
is Jesus the Son of *Allah*?

The question is not about Jesus, but *Allah*:
The Arabic for God is more than a name
but is He the same
as our God and Father?

In Southern Sudan
a Christian will answer, militantly, 'No':
in Pakistan
a Christian may answer, philosophically, 'Yes':
in Saudi Arabia
a Muslim will answer, immediately, 'No':
so does it depend where we stand – or kneel?

*El Shaddai* of Abraham
is revealed as *Yahweh* to Moses,
but not as *Ba'al* to Elijah:
what of Almighty *Allah*?

The crucial clue may lead us to
a Muslim now submitting

to the Ultimate Submitter,
Jesus the Messiah.

He does not change his God,
for God is One,
but discovers in the Son
that God is strangely, inconceivably great,
because He became so conceivably small;
that God, in the end, is mercifully just,
since He has absorbed the evil of all.

We may, perhaps, then whisper
that Jesus is the Son of *Allah*:
but in this naked act of naming,
the active Word transforms the Name.

Prostrate upon the carpet of a Mombasa mosque,
softly to Jesus, Son of 'Allah', I prayed;
then rose again to slip outside
and join my wife and daughters,
who were waiting in the shade.

To avoid misunderstanding – and the subject is obviously controversial – it may help to add some contextual comments on the text of the poem. It is important to realize that the Arabic word 'Allah' predates Islam and is used today as the word for 'God' by the Coptic Church of Egypt. Different countries are mentioned, where the ratios of Christians to Muslims vary: Sudan, Pakistan and Saudi Arabia. The heart of the poem considers the question of 'continuity' between the concept of God in Islam and the 'God and Father of our Lord Jesus Christ'. Is the relationship one of 'continuity', like the relationship between the Mesopotamian High God 'El' (often with the added adjective 'Shaddai' – meaning 'Almighty') and the unique name revealed to Moses, 'Yahweh' (see Exodus 6.3)? Or is the relationship one of confrontation similar to Yahweh's confronting of Ba'al (the supreme fertility god of the Canaanites) through Elijah's prophetic miracles (see 1 Kings 18.20–40)? Or is there a more subtle answer?

The 'cross-like' clue of an answer comes from thinking about a Muslim who has become a Christian – something that happened to Abdul Masih in 1810 and to countless other people over the centuries. One of the root meanings of the word 'Muslim' is 'one who submits'. Islam has always claimed Abraham as a Muslim, because he submitted to God. Using this meaning, the poem presents Jesus Christ as the complete 'Muslim' – the 'Ultimate Submitter' – in the sense that he, alone, has fully submitted to God in life (John 7.16–18), and particularly in death (Mark 14.32–42).

It seems to me that there is indeed continuity of the concept of God for the Muslim who becomes a Christian, for God is One, but also paradoxical new insights come through Jesus Christ – who really was crucified, and not replaced by another at the last moment, as mentioned in the Qur'an. God in his Son enters his own created world and, in the crucified Christ, takes away, and into himself, the sin of that world. Thereby, the conflicting Islamic adjectives for Allah, 'merciful' and 'just', are reconciled.

This continuity is recognized, although the word 'perhaps' in the poem shows hesitancy about the consequent mixing of different 'languages registers' between Islam and Christianity. The answer, however, is so horrific to Muslim ears that it can only be whispered, not shouted.

I refer to this daring and dangerous juxtaposition of three concepts, 'Jesus', 'Allah' and 'Allah having a Son', as a 'naked act of naming'. The Logos (the Word), who was in the beginning with God (John 1.1–4), is so powerful that the inner meaning of the name 'Allah' is actively changed into something like 'Abba', the Aramaic way of addressing God that was introduced by Jesus.

In realizing this, I had to change my posture in prayer to one that was more appropriate. I secretly enunciated the new insights by praying to Jesus as the Son of 'Allah', and then quietly left. After the continuity and transformation of the name, I rejoined my wife and daughters outside, and noted the contrast in attitudes to women. They were the first witnesses of the risen Jesus, but in Islam are kept in the shadows.

In the Old Testament, the Jewish understanding of God develops from one of his being 'only for us, the Jews' – our God is one God among many gods – to being 'unique for the whole world' – in other words, there is, in fact, only one God, and the other so-called gods do not actually exist. The key moment for this development was the recognition that God's rule was universal. The prophets who spoke and wrote during the exile of the Jews in Babylon, in the sixth century BC (e.g. Isaiah 45.20–25), declared that God had not been defeated by other gods – for they did not actually exist – but had judged his own people through the destruction executed by the army of Babylon.

So uniqueness (there is only one God) was declared in the context of universality (. . . and he rules everywhere, even in Babylon). The experience of being forced to live in another land, and later, the joyful return, led to a much wider and more powerful concept of God's just and saving rule.

A key passage of the New Testament concerning the question of what we have to share with people of other faiths is Acts 17.16–34. Have a look at it. Paul is waiting for Silas and Timothy to come to Athens, the capital of Greece and centre of philosophy and religion. One Roman satirist said that it was easier to find a god in Athens than a man! Paul does not waste his time, for the large-scale idolatry 'deeply distressed' him (v. 16). This is the word used in the Greek Old Testament translation to describe Yahweh's reaction to idolatry.

Paul engages in both dialogue evangelism and in proclamation. As usual, the gospel comes 'to the Jew first', in the synagogues, then Paul continues in the market place (like a sort of Christian Socrates), and ends up in the centre of power and intellect at the Areopagus, the council chamber. The word 'argued' (v. 17) can also be translated 'discussed persuasively'. It is not a monologue, but a dialogue aiming at conversion. The Epicurean philosophers (v. 18) are materialistic and have no belief in the afterlife, or even really in the gods. They emphasize reliance on the sense, elimination of superstition and pleasure as the only 'good'. The Stoics stress the importance of reason, right conduct and virtue and see God as the 'World Soul'. Some of Paul's writings echo Stoic ethics (e.g. Philippians 4.8). He is insulted and misunderstood. Some understand 'Jesus' to be the male god and 'resurrection' to be the female god, Jesus' wife (v. 18, where the Greek word for 'resurrection' is feminine).

Luke, the author of Acts as well as of his Gospel, gives us a fine literary summary of Paul's speech. Paul is addressing Gentiles, and so preaches in the appropriate style and does not quote the Old Testament. Starting from the known and moving to the unknown is good educational theory, and Paul does this by mentioning a particular altar and quoting with approval from the Greeks' own philosophical poets (Aratos and Epimenides, v. 28). Yet, more fundamentally, Paul is moving in the opposite direction – from the unknown to the Known. He presents to them the one true God: the Creator (v. 24), Sustainer (v. 25), Ruler of the Nations (v. 26), Father (vv. 28–29) and Judge (vv. 30–31). The specific mention of Jesus and the resurrection produces a mixture of mockery, interest and also definite converts. The person of Jesus focuses the message and brings decisive responses – one way or another.

But what about God's salvation in Jesus and people of other faiths? If Jesus is the unique Saviour, can only Christians be saved? This is one of the deepest questions of theology that people are asking today. I have noticed that people tend to take up one of four positions, which I outline below. In my description of them, the phrase 'the proclaimed Christ' includes the sensitive, integrated sharing of the good news of Jesus Christ by word and deed, and the word 'salvation' assumes the importance of temporal salvation in this life – though the focus in this discussion is on 'eternal salvation' beyond death. Although the four positions are outlined for clarity, in reality the boundaries are often blurred. Not all Christians can be fitted neatly into one of these positions, for many are reticent about such ultimate beliefs.

First, the 'narrow scope of salvation' position. In this understanding, salvation is centred on Jesus Christ for those who respond in faith to the proclaimed Christ and eternal punishment in hell is expected for those who have never heard of Christ, and for those who reject the proclaimed Christ. Very conservative Christians, of many traditions, hold to this 'narrow scope'. However, in effect, it seems to involve the doctrine of what could be termed 'condemnation by geography or time'. If you were born outside of an area where, or before the time when, the good news of Christ had been effectively proclaimed you would be automatically condemned on the last day. Thus God's eternal purpose would be dependent on historical contingency – where and when you were born. To me, this does not seem to match the criteria of the justice of God. Paul argues in Romans that God is just, even on terms of human justice.

Second, the 'wider hope of salvation' stance. In this understanding, salvation is centred on Jesus Christ for those who respond in faith to the proclaimed Christ and for those who respond in faith to 'God' *as they know him*. Judgement into eternal nothingness is expected for those who reject the proclaimed Christ or 'God' *as they know him*. As we saw in Chapter 1, hell therefore is not eternal punishment by God, but 'de-creation' by him, back into the nothingness out of which he originally summoned creation. This seems to me to make most sense. This position holds to the reality of eternal judgement, but tries to avoid the twin injustices of eternal punishment (by holding to the doctrine of 'de-creation') and of 'condemnation by geography and time' (by stressing the validity of the open response of faith in 'God' as he is already known, before the good news is proclaimed). In Acts chapter 10, the situation of Cornelius, a Roman Centurion who was open in faith to God, is interesting. Peter says on meeting him and hearing his story, 'I truly understand that God shows no partiality' (v. 34). Cornelius is described as a devout man who feared God (v. 2) and who was upright (v. 22). God answered his prayers (v. 4) and Peter says that he was *acceptable* to God (v. 35). This is the key word (see its other uses in Luke 4.19 and 4.24, 2 Corinthians 6.2, and Philippians 4.18). It implies that, although before Peter came he was not part of the people of God, nor did he have the Holy Spirit, Cornelius would have been welcomed into God's kingdom if he had died before hearing the gospel from Peter. God sees deep into people's hearts, as to whether they are open in faith to him or not.

Third, there is the 'cosmic promise of salvation'. In this understanding, universal salvation is for all, centred on Christ, for those who respond in faith to the proclaimed Christ, for those who respond in faith to 'God' as they know him, *and for those who reject* the proclaimed Christ or 'God' as they know him. There is judgement in time (in this life), but no eternal judgement. People who believe this sometimes betray an uneasy ambivalence about the biblical passages that denote judgement for eternity. Concerning this position, it may be questioned whether the warnings of Jesus and of Paul are taken seriously enough. It may claim to be strong on grace but, in effect, may be weak on human responsibility.

Finally, the 'natural assumption of salvation' position. In this understanding, universal salvation is for all, *centred on 'God', with Jesus as merely a human prophet.* There is no judgement in time, nor in eternity. This position seems to involve a radical reinterpretation of the doctrine of God, cutting loose from Christian understandings of the divinity of Christ, which, in effect, cries out for a new religion. It appears to be weak on biblical analysis, which is seen as less important than philosophical considerations.

From my study of the Bible, wider reading and conversations in Kenya, Cambridge and London, the second position – of 'wider hope' – seems to me to be the most authentic. It is based on the openness of faith in God as he is known at that point, wherever and whenever the person may be born. In Romans chapter four, Paul shows how Abraham's faith in God illustrates, and is equated with, our faith in Christ. Jesus said that he was 'the only way to the Father' (John 14.6), and yet clearly Abraham is saved. Abraham therefore must 'come to the Father' through Christ (there is no other way) and comes by faith (there really is no other way). His faith in God is counted as faith in God and in Jesus Christ.

Some people react to the plurality of religions today as if it were a new situation, and begin to doubt the 'uniqueness' of Jesus Christ. Christianity was born among many religions and would not have spread without the definite belief in Christ's 'uniqueness' and 'universality'. The two go together inextricably. In sharing the good news with people of other faiths, including those of 'New Age spiritualities', it would be good to follow Paul's example of versatility, sensitivity, dialogue, proclamation, use of their sacred writings, and specific mention of Jesus.

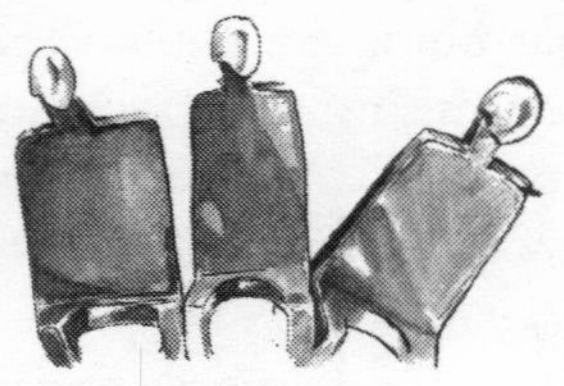

# Suffering

## LENT

### Why do some children suffer while others are blessed?

The word 'Lent' in English comes from the 'lengthening' of the hours of daylight. The season emanated from the preparation of people for baptism in the early Church, when Easter was the time for baptism. It was also the time of confessing the reality of wrongdoing for those who had been excommunicated from the Church for serious sins.

This specific period of time developed into a season for all Christians to focus on preparing for Easter. The context for considering sins was shaped through the triple themes of giving money, prayer and fasting. Jesus, in the Sermon on the Mount, assumed all three are important: 'when you give money . . . when you pray . . . when you fast . . . ' (Matthew 6.1–18).

Later there developed the tradition of meditation on Jesus' time in the wilderness, tempted by the evil one. I remember being struck by a key point on this made by George Caird of Oxford in his 1963 Penguin commentary on Luke – the most beautifully succinct and perceptive book on a Gospel I have ever read. I return to it again and again, so much so that my copy is falling apart. Caird stressed that temptation aims at our strong points, not at our weaknesses:

> A man of fervent dedicated spirit, feeling himself called to liberate the oppressed and to establish the reign of justice and peace, would be open to three types of temptation: to allow the good to usurp the place of the best, to seek God's ends by means alien to God's character, and to force God's hand by taking short cuts to success. And these are the three temptations of Jesus.

Have a look at Luke 4.1–13, with the temptations to provide bread for himself (and by extension for everyone), to take political power to bring in the kingdom of God, and to test God with a miracle (which could be taken to be a trick leading to death). Caird continued:

> Each of these three temptations attacked Jesus not at a point of weakness but at his greatest strength – his compassion, his commitment and his faith.

So, an unusual biblical way of taking Lent seriously would be to consider our strong points and how they can be turned towards evil.

As well as evil coming from people giving way to temptation, there are all kinds of tragic suffering that afflict the innocent. Have a look at the photo of the sculpture by Jonathan Clarke. It is called 'Christ blessing the Children' and is, in fact, a lectern with a book rest at the back of it, attached to the figure of Christ. The book rest can be moved up and down at various levels, to adjust to the height of the person reading. When a young child is reading, Christ is at the level of the figures facing him and he is blessing them. When it is raised, as in the photo, the scenario changes from Christ blessing the children to Christ ascending to heaven and the figures facing him become the disciples.

You can't see it on the photo, but on the front of the smallest child, right in the centre facing towards Christ, is the letter H. This is the clue to the whole sculpture. Harvey was a little baby who died tragically from an illness at the age of three months. His parents, Karl and Carrie, live near St Mary's Church and after the funeral they said that they would like to have some sort of memorial to Harvey in the church. I suggested we met with an artist friend, Jonathan Clarke, who travelled down from his studio near Bury St Edmunds to meet the

'Christ Blessing the Children', Jonathan Clarke.
(See colour section)

three of us. Jonathan produced a sketch which was agreed and then a model, before finally casting it. Karl and Carrie arranged a memorial party for their community, and people who live in the area, but who don't usually come to church, contributed towards the memorial fund.

Jonathan carves in polystyrene, the material often used for packing computers and televisions. He moves a block of polystyrene around an electric hot wire, cutting out a shape. Then he buries it in Warwickshire sand – a particular type of sand that packs up closely to the mould – and pours molten aluminium into the mould through a hole at the top of the sand. The polystyrene vaporizes and the aluminium takes its form. Each sculpture is unique, since the mould is lost and cannot be used again. Great care has to be taken during the delicate moment of pouring. If something goes wrong then, the sculptor has to begin all over again.

Have a look at the photo again. It was taken by Victor Virdi, a professional photographer whose faith in Christ came alive on an Alpha course at our church. He spent the whole morning in church taking different shots of the sculpture in natural daylight. When we looked at the photos together, we spotted the power of this particular one. Can you see the shadow of Christ's left arm forming, by chance, a point in his side? It reminded us of the sword that pierced his side on the cross (John 19.34).

So the sculpture and the photographic study of it have several layers of meaning behind them: the tragedy of a baby's death, memory, bereavement of the parents, solidarity of community support and imaginative creation. The theological themes include Christ welcoming children, the ascension and the cross.

This is appropriate, really, since Jesus said, 'whoever does not receive the kingdom of God as a little child will never enter it' (Mark 10.15). The context of that verse is the passage Mark 10.13–16. Parents are bringing their children to Jesus for a tangible blessing as Jacob (whose other name was Israel) blessed his grandsons, the sons of Joseph (Genesis 48.13–14). The rebuke of Jesus' 'minders' was presumably to save him the time and bother, but Jesus is cross with his disciples and his command not to 'hinder' or 'prevent' them seems to have become part of the language of the baptism service in the early Church.

Babies and children are in the best position for understanding what it means to be a child of God. It is rather obvious when we think about it. They have nothing to earn and show for themselves and are not embarrassed to receive presents openly. Motives for giving are not questioned. With his characteristic, astounding authority – 'Truly I say to you . . .' – which belongs to God alone (see Mark 2.5–7), Jesus declares the presence of the longed-for kingdom now. He embodies the kingdom himself and embraces the children. The word 'bless' has emphasis – he blessed them fervently.

Mark was probably writing in Rome, and Jesus' attitude to babies and children is in sharp contrast to the practice of exposing unwanted babies, especially girls, that was common in various parts of the Empire. In the mission of the Church, this passage has inspired the setting up of countless Christian orphanages.

Jesus, who blesses the little children, had once been a child himself – 'Tears and smiles like us he knew' (from the carol 'Once in Royal

David's City') is much more realistic, and orthodox, than 'the little Lord Jesus no crying he makes' (from 'Away in a Manger'). We touched on the importance of this in Chapter 2 and mentioned the verse Luke 2.52 concerning Jesus' growth as a child. The whole passage in which that verse is set is worth looking at – Luke 2.41–52.

A Jewish boy becomes a 'son of the Law', bar mitzvah, at the age of 13, taking on the obligations to which circumcision committed him. Jews were meant to go to Jerusalem three times a year, but Jesus' parents were poor and lived at a distance. So they went annually at Passover, the seven-day feast celebrating the escape from Egypt. Communal life meant that Jesus' absence from the caravan of Galilean pilgrims was not noticed at first. Imagine the anxious pain of his parents during the three days of searching. They knew he was special and precious, and yet now he was lost. Abraham might have had such despairing feelings when he was commanded to sacrifice his promised son Isaac. The word describing the anguish experienced by Mary and Joseph is used by Luke in Acts 20.38 for the feelings of the Ephesian Christians when saying a final farewell to Paul. Yet Jesus was safe and in the obvious place. The teachers of the law were astounded at his insight, and later they were affronted on this same spot (Luke 20.1–2).

The concept of God as the father of his son Israel is found in the Hebrew Scriptures, even though God is not addressed as 'Father' prior to Jesus' specific way of praying. For the first time in Luke's Gospel, even before his baptism (and perhaps in response to the mention of Joseph?), Jesus refers to his distinctively intimate relationship to God his Father. 'My Father's house' can also be translated 'my Father's business (or affairs)'. Luke records that Mary kept all these things in her heart (see also Luke 2.19). Perhaps she was Luke's special source for these stories.

I began the notes for the following poem beside a swimming pool in Brittany, during a family holiday in 1996. It has the parallel themes of both a woman giving birth and the various aspects of 'water' in the Bible, from beginning to end. It has been used in contexts of freedom as well as of bereavement.

## By the Waters of Delivery

By breathing and brooding,
by breaking and birthing,
by parting and loosing,
by stirring and soothing:

by giving, re-living,
by stilling, refreshing,
by drowning, immersing,
by raising, re-versing,
you, Lord, deliver us.

The 'breathing and brooding' echoes the Spirit in Genesis 1.1–2. The 'breaking and birthing, parting and loosing' remembers the parting of the Red Sea and the birth of the nation, released from bondage in Egypt (Exodus 14). In the New Testament, the 'stirring and soothing' points to the pool of Bethzatha (John 5.1–9) where Jesus healed a lame man, and 'giving, re-living' refers to Jesus meeting the woman of Samaria (John 4. 7–42, especially v. 10). 'Stilling, refreshing' hints at both Psalm 23 ('beside still waters; he restores my soul') and Jesus stilling the storm on Lake Galilee (Mark 4.35–41).

'Drowning, immersing' and 'raising, re-versing' refers to our dying with Christ in the waters of baptism and being raised with him to new life here, and eventual resurrection in the age to come (Romans 6.1–11). The word 're-versing' deliberately echoes both the turning back of death, in the transformation of resurrection, and a variant meaning of the Greek word *poiema* of Ephesians 2.10: 'For we are God's *handiwork* [my italic], created in Christ Jesus . . .' (NEB and REB translations). This Greek word was applied to a range of action from work on physical material to the composing of poetry. The Oxford English Dictionary entry for 'poem' states: 'Greek *poema*, early variant of *poiema*, thing made or created, work, fiction, poetical work'. So, the concept of this particular line in the poem implies that in our new life in Christ, and ultimately in the resurrection, we are 're-poemed' as well as delivered – quite a thought.

But, again, what about those who are *not* delivered in this life, and who, for example, innocently get blown up on a Number 30 bus on 7 July 2005 (that bus route is local to me in that it passes both the British Library and St Mary's Church in Islington), or drowned in the Asian tsunami of 26 December 2004? What about them? Terrorists were to blame for the London bombings, but is God also to blame? Children, as well as others, died by drowning in Sri Lanka and Indonesia in that so-called 'natural disaster' – what had they done to deserve it? Again, where was God?

Various false ideas of God surfaced after the tragic Asian tsunami, and it would be good to focus our discussion on a particular event. First, the idea of the *vindictive god*: he is seen as punishing the sins of people in Indonesia, Thailand and Sri Lanka. Jesus' own words speak against such a view: '. . . those eighteen who were killed when the tower of Siloam fell on them – do you think that they were worse offenders than all the others living in Jerusalem?' (Luke 13.1–5).

Second, the false idea of the *absentee god* – in other words, that he set the world going but does not intervene in it again. This seems like a firework instruction: light the blue touch-paper and retire. As we saw in Chapter 1, God does not retire. He did create, continues to do so, and is still deeply involved in his creation.

Third, there is the false idea of the *puppet-master god*. Some think the world is like the Little Angel Puppet Theatre, just behind St Mary's Church in Islington: he created the world and now intervenes in every single aspect. But we have been given freedom and God is not manipulative. Rowan Williams has commented: 'There is something odd about expecting that God will constantly step in if things get dangerous. How dangerous do they have to be? How many deaths would be acceptable?'

Fourth, the false idea of the *tribal god*: he loves only Christians and was punishing Muslims in Indonesia and Buddhists in Sri Lanka. But we can see that Jesus' loving attitude to the Samaritans of his day puts that great lie to rest (John 4 and Luke 10).

Finally, there is the *calculating god* viewpoint – some thought he was showing us the imminent end of the world in the tsunami. Jesus did warn of earthquakes and wars, and God will one day wrap up history and recreate the whole universe, but Jesus did also warn against predicting particular times.

Christians believe in a creator God who is still creating, and is intimately involved in his work. Paul wrote to the church at Rome: 'We know that the whole creation has been groaning in labour pains until now; and not only creation, but we ourselves, who have the first fruits of the Spirit, groan inwardly.' Many saw this echoed in the tragic tsunami. Later Paul mentioned the Spirit groaning within us, helping us in our weakness in prayer (Romans 8.22–23, 26). So there is a triple groaning.

During Radio 4's 'Thought for the Day' on 29 December 2004, following the devastating tsunami, Elaine Storkey commented perceptively: 'There will be movements of tectonic plates, there will be serious earthquakes along the San Andreas Fault and with devastating effects. This is not a limitation of God's power or love but a description of the world we live in: a world not yet fully delivered and longing for cosmic redemption.'

We also believe in a participating God, Father, Son and Holy Spirit, and perhaps there is a danger of leaving Christ out of our concept of God when we ponder these deep questions? We saw above the significance of baptism in terms of drowning. God, through his Son, entered his own creation and suffered innocently on the cross, and his baptism foreshadowed that cross. He did not need to be baptized, but went under the water for us. Some may say, 'If God created the world, then he should pay for its suffering.' Christians can only point towards the cross, and it is to the cross that we now move.

# Dying

## GOOD FRIDAY

### How can one death affect the lives of so many?

Woody Allen once remarked, 'It's not that I'm afraid to die, it's just that I don't want to be there at the time.' Many Christians also feel like that, but the heart of our belief is that Christ has indeed been there. He died because death could only be destroyed from the inside, not the outside. There really is no other way. The effect of that particular death depended on the identity of the one who died. It was unique because Jesus was, and is, unique. Irony is embedded in the name 'Good Friday': in the Orthodox Church it is called 'Great Friday'.

Have a look at the photo of another sculpture by Jonathan Clarke, 'The Eighth Hour'. I first saw it at his studio home near Bury St Edmund's on the Wednesday of Holy Week, 2000. He had wandered into The Gallery art shop in Aldeburgh on the Suffolk coast the previous Monday, just as I was asking the owner about a work of art for our home. The owner said, 'Jonathan's best work is languishing in his basement. It was commissioned by me as a parish priest before I left that particular parish to take up my new venture of The Gallery. My successor did not follow up the project.' From the description, I was fascinated, saying to Jonathan that I needed a visual image for my

Good Friday sermon later in the week at St Andrew's Church, Chesterton, Cambridge.

The Eighth Hour depicts the hour before Jesus died. His body is of aluminium and the cross is of rough oak. His body is not so much on the cross as *in* it. He *is* the cross, and the wooden arms of the cross are his arms and the wooden base his legs. I asked if I could borrow the sculpture for my sermon and then look after it for a period of time, and he agreed. We carefully took off the top of the sculpture and put the base and the top in the boot of my car. I drove home at 30 miles an hour, feeling as if I had a body in the back of the car.

Back home, my wife Alison, our daughter Miriam, and I set it up in the corner of our main room and gazed at it for over an hour, ideas flowing quietly and gently. After a while, one of us noted a skull shape skewed in the body – and we remembered the hill of Golgotha, 'the place of the skull'. We saw three twists in the arms of the cross, which are the arms of Christ. The edges of the arms are twisted upwards from the line of the horizontal, backwards from a line running across the front from left to right, and they are out of line with each other, somewhat similar to a Rubik's cube.

'The Eighth Hour', Jonathan Clarke. (See colour section)

For Good Friday the following year, when we had moved to Islington, we had a large poster of the sculpture outside St Mary's Church, facing Upper Street. People were intrigued, and someone asked me why we had a close-up photo of helicopter wings. I asked him to look again. He was deeply moved on seeing it afresh and said, 'I used to be a helicopter pilot. Do you know what we call the pin that holds the blades on to the main body of the helicopter? If that fails, it crashes.' I said that I didn't know what the pin was called. He replied, 'It's called the Jesus pin' – because this was the cry of despair that went up if it failed. I pointed him to Paul's words that in Christ 'all things hold together' (Colossians 1.17).

This sculpture shows a muscular Christ. He seems to me to be aggressively taking on the evil of the world. He resembles, perhaps, Samson, the Israelite hero. His arms could be seen as pushing out the pillars of the Philistine pagan temple. Or perhaps the evil of the world is encroaching on him. He is pushing – and at the same time being constrained and constricted (see Luke 8.45 and 12.50). There is a powerful verse in the Samson story that says, 'So those he killed at his death were more than those he had killed during his life' (Judges 16.30). Jesus accomplishes the reverse of that. He saves more people through his death than he was able to save during his life. But saved from what, and how?

The cross confronts us with the issue of sin. Sin is tyrannous, terrifying and addictive: we are ruled by it, live in fear of its power, and can't get out of its grip on our attention. Particular sins are enumerated in the Ten Commandments (Exodus 20.1–17), and summarized in Jesus' double commandment of loving God and neighbour (Mark 12.29–31), which echoed contemporary discussions in Judaism. I was struck recently how similar the first and last commandments of the Ten Commandments are to Jesus' summary of them. He seems to be 'book-ending' the Ten Commandments by picking on the first and the last and turning them into positive statements.

The first commandment is, 'You shall have no other gods before me', and Jesus puts this positively and lovingly by quoting Deuteronomy 6.5, 'You shall love the Lord your God with all your heart, and with all your soul, and with all your mind, and with all your strength'

(Mark 12.30). The last commandment is, 'You shall not covet your neighbour's house; you shall not covet your neighbour's wife, or male or female slave, or ox or donkey, or anything that belongs to your neighbour.' The word 'neighbour' is repeated three times, and this, perhaps, is the clue. Jesus again puts that positively and lovingly by quoting Leviticus 19.6, 'You shall love your neighbour as yourself' (Mark 12.31).

So the essence of sin is not loving God and not loving your neighbour. Sins of omission are as serious as sins of commission. The passage in Luke's Gospel concerning the summary of the law continues with the lawyer's question – typical really – 'And who is my neighbour?', which evokes from Jesus the parable of the Good Samaritan. 'Passing by on the other side' may be the archetypal sin of omission, but others involve procrastination – 'putting off till tomorrow what is needed to be done today'. I love this anonymous rhyme:

Procrastination is my sin,
It brings me greatest sorrow;
I really must stop doing it,
I think I'll start tomorrow.

The kingdom of God preached by Jesus is the opposite of this sin, for in his ministry and announcement of justice, 'tomorrow breaks into today'. The longed for 'Last Day' has arrived and Scripture is fulfilled (Luke 4.21). Donald Nicholl, author of *Holiness*, has perceptively focused the essence of holiness as 'doing the next right thing'.

Perhaps another way of understanding sin, and God's response to it on the cross, is to consider the stories where Jesus is angry. This is an interesting concept. Jesus is usually angry with sin and its tyranny, rather than with sinners, who flock to hear him and, indeed, party with him. But sometimes he is angry with those who perpetrate sin. He is certainly angry with religious hypocrisy (Matthew 23), with its wrecking of the Temple's purpose (Mark 11), and also with leprosy deforming someone made in the image of God (Mark 1.40–45). There is a fascinating variant reading in the margins of Mark 1.41 which states that Jesus was angry. This could wrongly imply that he was angry with the leper, but I think he was angry with the leprosy. Other manuscripts, perhaps wary of this misunderstanding, have the Greek word meaning 'moved with compassion'. The Revised English Bible tries to have the best of both worlds – and falls between two stools – with its translation 'with warm indignation': but I think the full force of Jesus' anger with leprosy messing up someone's life should not be watered down. A person made in the image of God should not be so deformed, and it was not so at the beginning.

Was God the Father cross at the cross – with this ultimate sin, the killing of his Son? Yes, I think he was furious with the concentrated, focused sin of the world. He was angry with the perpetrators of the execution of his beloved Son, which included the manipulation of the leaders of the Jews, the fickleness of the mob, and the cowardice of Pontius Pilate.

In John chapters 18 and 19 we see the confrontation of sheer political power and eternal glory arraigned and arrayed in weakness. Where, then, is real power and who is ultimately on trial, Jesus or Pilate? The contrast is between Gabbatha and Golgotha – the Pavement, where Pilate's trial of Jesus takes place (John 19.13), and the Skull, where Jesus is executed (John 19.17). Pilate reigns on Gabbatha and Jesus reigns from Golgotha. Francis Bacon's most famous essay, 'On Truth', begins, 'What is truth? said jesting Pilate; and would not stay for an answer.' In fact, Truth is standing before him. Pilate is solid and seated. Jesus is weak and standing. Jesus is dangled three times by Pilate: first in front of the leaders of the Jews, then before the crowd and finally on the cross.

Of the four Gospels we have in the New Testament, the Gospel of Mark is considered to be the first one to have been written. Early on Good Friday in 1999, however, I noticed that the plaque that Pontius Pilate had ordered for the cross (John 19.19–22) may in fact deserve that title.

## First Written Gospel

Jesus the Sacred, tried before Pilate;
Pilate, the scared – trial before Caesar?
Jesus, entitled to justice from Rome,
entitled by Pilate, 'The King of the Jews'.

First written Gospel, translated for all,
title deeds of the kingdom of God;
proclaimed to the city, unchanging Word,
'What is written, is written', bequeathed to the world.

How did the particular death of Jesus of Nazareth save billions of people across the ages and across the world? There are a whole series of metaphors used in the New Testament to explore that question, and they are like a multifaceted jewel. We will now look at three faces of this jewel: substitution, victory and ransom.

Various modern illustrations of substitution and the cross have been offered, and some of them, frankly, raise more moral questions than they attempt to solve. Perhaps it may be better to draw on two passages in the Gospel of John:

> Caiaphas, who was high priest that year, said to [the Sanhedrin Council], 'You know nothing at all! You do not understand that it is better for you to have one man die for the people than to have the whole nation destroyed.' (John 11.49–50)

The writer of this Gospel then elucidates the ironic, divine inspiration of Caiaphas' cynical statement and widens it to include the Gentiles:

> He did not say this on his own, but being high priest that year he prophesied that Jesus was about to die for the nation, and not for the nation only, but to gather into one the dispersed children of God. (John 11.51–52)

So 'substitution' is written deep into the story of the cross. At the end of John chapter 18 we meet Barabbas, who is described as a 'bandit'. A 'guerrilla fighter' may be more accurate – he was a 'zealot' who wanted to rid Palestine of the Romans. There was a custom that the Roman Governor could release one prisoner at the Passover festival. Pontius Pilate offered to release Jesus, but the crowd called for Barabbas. His Aramaic name means 'son of the father', which seems to mimic Jesus' particular relationship to God. Barabbas, who deserves to be executed, is set free, and Jesus, the unique Son of the Father, who committed no wrong, dies in his place. So Barabbas is the model for us who deserve to die for our sins, but are released because another took our place.

Instead of a response of love towards God and our neighbour, sin involves putting ourselves in the place of God and of our neighbour. The extraordinary good news of the cross is that God in Christ has put himself in the place of us and of our neighbour.

In terms of the metaphor of victory, sin is fought and destroyed strangely by absorption. Jesus on the cross was actively taking on the evil of the universe. He took it on in a double sense. Taking it into himself, he took it out of circulation: instead of passing it on, he absorbed it. He also took it on in terms of confronting it. Here is the wrestling. Here is the fight. Here is the war on the tyranny, terror and addiction of sin. Christ is face to face with evil on the cross. The irony is that evil appears to have won. But the personifications of evil and terror, sin and death overreach themselves, boasting of their victory. Just at the moment of defeat, they are routed by the route of the cross.

In Tolkien's powerful, multi-layered, myth-making trilogy *The Lord of the Rings*, the ring may be seen as a symbol of tyranny, terror and addiction. It can only be destroyed by taking it to the place where it was first formed, Mount Doom, and dropping it into the abyss at the centre of the mountain. Even the heroic hobbit, Frodo, cannot bring himself to let it go at the crucial moment and his finger, with the ring on it, is bitten off by Gollum. Gollum falls into the abyss and the ring is destroyed for ever. Strangely, on Good Friday we see that the place of God's frightening love is the cross. In the story of Genesis, sin came into the world through Adam, the first man. Paul shows, in Romans 5.12–21, how it could only be dealt with by a 'second' Adam, the ultimate man. The end of sin matches its beginning and the importance of the full humanity of Christ is again recognized. On the cross, sin is consigned to the abyss of the body of Christ and destroyed by absorption.

Our third metaphor, ransom, is rooted in Jesus' words: 'For the Son of Man came not to be served but to serve, and to give his life a ransom for many' (Mark 10.45). The Greek word translated 'for' in that verse is a strong word that means 'instead of' – which relates to our first metaphor of substitution. It may seem at first sight to be anachronistic to our modern world, but this payment to set slaves free is still evocative and controversial today, particularly in the questions surrounding hostage deals.

In the autumn term of 1992, I had a sabbatical at Yale University, and during that time Terry Waite came to speak to the students. He had been kept as a hostage by militant Islamists in Beirut for four years, mostly in solitary confinement. No deal was made in his case, but I meditated on this concept of a hostage and the narrative of Jesus at the tomb of his friend Lazarus (John 11.1–44). I wrote the following poem soon after his visit. It combines within it the metaphors we have been considering of substitution, victory through absorption and ransom.

## The Hostage Deal

Between the rolling of the stone
   and the crying of the name
   came the agonizing.
Shuddering, Jesus stares into the tomb,
Making a deal with death in the depths.
A greedy exchange is strangely agreed:
Lazarus comes out and he will go in,
The prize of life for the price of death.

The hour of starkness fully come,
The Dealer is struck and laid in the tomb.

Then is the end, but the end is of death:
Through terrifying life in the depths,
Death is destroyed, exploded inside.

Before the rolling of the stone
  and the coming of the women
  came the rising.

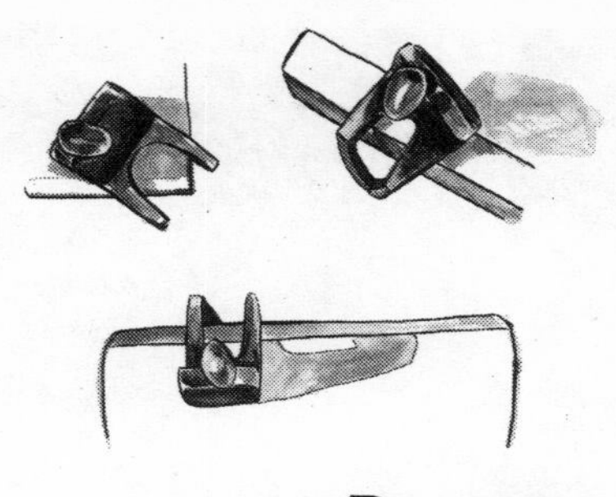

# Rising

## EASTER

### Is there anything more to life than this?

Sidney Smith, a great clerical wit, saw two women arguing from two tall buildings across the street in Edinburgh. 'They'll never agree,' he said. 'They're arguing from different premises.' The premise of Christian theology is that Jesus was raised from the dead on the third day.

Death was exploded from the inside by the resurrection of Jesus Christ. At the cross, sin was conquered by absorption. At the resurrection, death was destroyed by explosion.

There are two particular misinterpretations of the story of Easter which truncate its radical good news. The first denies the resurrection of the 'body' of Jesus, insisting instead on merely a 'spiritual' rising, with the resurrection appearances demoted to spiritual apparitions. This is questioned by the importance that the Gospels give to the significance of the empty tomb – there really was no body left there at all – and also by Paul's emphasis on the burial of Jesus' body (1 Corinthians 15.3–4 and Romans 6.1–4). Matter *does* matter eternally.

The second misinterpretation ignores the difference between resuscitation from death, which led back into ordinary life in Palestine, and

'Rabbouni', Silvia Dimitrova. (See colour section)

resurrection from the dead, which led forward into glorious new life in heaven and which also included a series of appearances by Jesus to his disciples for their encouragement. Lazarus, and others in the Gospels who were raised back to life from death by Jesus, still had to die again. Jesus did not. He was raised by his Father, by the power of the Spirit, into glorious new life in community – body, mind and spirit.

Have a look at the photo of Silvia Dimitrova's painting 'Rabbouni'. In 2002, I saw Silvia's paintings of egg tempera on wood at an exhibition at the Business Design Centre, Islington. From my meeting with her came the first exhibition in our Crypt Gallery in May 2003 called 'Sacred and Secular', which showed her traditional Bulgarian icons and modern Bulgarian folk pictures, depicting mostly love scenes. The quotation advertising the exhibition was from Kenneth Cragg, a Christian scholar of Islam: 'The sacred is the destiny of the secular and the secular is the raw material of the sacred.'

Silvia trained as a Bulgarian Orthodox icon painter and her studio is currently at Downside, the Roman Catholic Abbey and boarding school in Somerset. Downside invited her over from Bulgaria to paint an icon of St Benedict and she married a lay schoolmaster, Simon, and stayed. In 2000 she was artist in residence at nearby Wells Cathedral and painted 14 stations of the cross for the millennium.

For my fiftieth birthday in 2003, Alison and I commissioned Silvia to paint the face of Mary Magdalene, as she heard Jesus call her name on Easter morning. I knew of many paintings of this famous encounter centred around Mary wanting to touch Jesus, but of none so far that had captured the very moment – a few seconds earlier – of Mary hearing her own name pronounced by her Teacher. We discussed the possibility of depicting that moment that her faith comes alive – her face of faith. Silvia asked me to read the passage from John 20.11–18 on to tape. She meditated on the text and the reading on the tape, prayed and painted. When she arrived with the painting, I was delighted with its beauty and shape; it was three times the size we expected. She had not only painted Mary, but also added Jesus, the angels, trees and the tomb.

In the story of John chapter 20, Mary Magdalene, devastated in her bereavement, mistakes Jesus for the gardener:

> Jesus said to her, 'Woman, why are you weeping? For whom are you looking?' Supposing him to be the gardener, she said to him, 'Sir, if you have carried him away, tell me where you have laid him, and I will take him away.' Jesus said to her, 'Mary!' She turned and said to him in Hebrew, 'Rabbouni!' (which means Teacher). (John 20.15–16)

## Rabbouni

Who is this woman facing this man?
Head lightly inclined,
eyes wide open, gazing;
hands uplifted, palms upward, surprised;
gorgeously arrayed.

Who is this man facing this woman?
Coming from the right,
profile clear, bearded;
hand outstretched, palm down;
gloriously appareled.

Behind her, two angels hover
reflecting her shape:
behind him, scented trees lean
setting the scene:
below her, a dark opening hints.
All silent witnesses.

The eyes have it:
focus of tension and attention.
One word awakes her: 'Mary'.
One word responds: 'Rabbouni'.

Their hands shape a triangle
at the centre of meeting:
her two, shocked and suppliant;
his one, blessing, calming, sending.

As Christians, we believe that one day we are going to live in the full, glorious presence of God. We cannot easily imagine what it will be like – the book of Revelation has symbols of harps, songs, psalms, crowns and white robes, which suggest joy and fulfilment. One thing we *do* know is that we cannot live in heaven with our current bodies. We need to be changed.

Have a look at 1 Corinthians 15.35–58. Paul is writing to the church he founded at Corinth. He says in verse 50, 'What I am saying, brothers and sisters, is this: flesh and blood cannot inherit the kingdom of God.' So what are our resurrection bodies going to be like?

First, climate change. We need to be transformed to enter a new climate. In winter, children and adults often enjoy making a snowman. When the thaw comes, however, the snowman dies and disappears. His body cannot cope with the new climate and our bodies cannot survive in the pure climate of God's heaven. Think about a baby. A foetus is tucked up in the womb and relies totally on the mother for life support. It has no idea of the enormity and diversity of real life, because it is restricted. Then, after a great traumatic experience, the baby is born. Immediately a new system for acquiring oxygen kicks in: the placenta process, through the mother, gives way to air directly sucked into the lungs.

Second, the characteristics of our new bodies. Whatever new environment God has thought of for his creatures, he has found precisely the appropriate body for them. Verses 39–40 mention feathers and wings for creatures in the sky, burning gases for outer space and resurrection bodies for eternity, which Paul describes, in verses 42–44, as imperishable, glorious, powerful and spirit-directed. They are imperishable because they cannot die again. This is not the 'immortality of the soul' – a Greek concept – but the resurrection of the body – the whole person, as conceived of in Hebrew thought. God did not negotiate a compromise agreement with death, in which death took the human body – and kept it – and God took the human spirit. No. Resurrection was a complete, not a partial, victory for God the creator. A body allows us to live, not just survive. Efficient ears enjoy music, good taste buds appreciate food. In heaven perhaps there may not be music by means of vibrating sound waves, but we may well be able to enjoy deeper, richer counterparts to music.

Our bodies will be glorious or beautiful. However we may feel when we look in the mirror now, however sin or events may have wrecked our current bodies, we will be transformed to be like his glorious body (see also Philippians 3.21). In a spiritual sense, we are already gradually being transformed from glory to glory (2 Corinthians 3.18), but our ultimate death and raising will be the focal point. Here our bodies are weak, but then they will be powerful and strong. Paul knew of the weakness of his body for he had been beaten, stoned and scourged for the sake of sharing the good news of Christ (2 Corinthians 11.24–29).

These new bodies will be 'directed by the spirit', which is a better translation than the usual one in verse 44 of a 'spiritual' body. The latter sounds somewhat like a wispy ghost. 'Spiritual' does not refer to what the body is made of, but how the body is controlled. Our natural or physical bodies are currently too often controlled by the 'flesh' rather than the 'spirit'. In heaven, we shall no longer have sinful inclinations but supernatural bodies under the direction of our spirits.

Third, a sample of the resurrection body. Paul writes in 1 Corinthians 15.20, 'But in fact Christ has been raised from the dead, the first fruits of those who have died.' There were similarities with his body before Good Friday, in that the marks of the nails and spear were recognizable and he ate fish with his disciples (John 20.26–29, and Luke 24.36–43), but there were also differences, in that he was able to appear in a room without walking through the door (John 20.19–23). A note of caution is perhaps worth considering, and that is that we only know the form of Christ's body in the Gospels when he was appearing to his disciples in this life. We would not expect that the full splendour of his heavenly glory could be communicated to his disciples who only saw with their earthly eyes. So the Gospels tell us some of the forms his body took, but not all of them. There will be much more for us to discover.

Fourth, when do we receive our resurrection bodies? This raises the question of the possibility of an intermediate state between death and the coming of Christ at the end of history. In the New Testament there are two strands that need to be brought together. The first implies that after death we are immediately with Christ. This is evidenced by Jesus' words to the guerrilla fighter on the cross – 'today you will be with me in Paradise' (Luke 23.39–43) – and by Paul's desire expressed to the Philippians that he would rather 'depart and be with Christ, for that is far better' (Philippians 1.20–26). The second implies that there will be a general resurrection of everyone on the last day (1 Thessalonians 4 and 1 Corinthians 15).

Three basic solutions have been offered to solve this tension. First, that after death we shall indeed be with Christ, but without our resurrection bodies. However, if this was the meaning, then why not put it more clearly? No indication is mentioned in the text of Luke or Philippians that being with Christ is only an intermediate state.

Second, the doctrine of what has been called 'soul sleep', which implies that we are unconsciously present with Christ. However, this does not take into account the vivid hope of Paul expressed in

Philippians 1.23. It also leans too heavily on the occasional metaphor of sleep in the New Testament used to represent death. Actually, the metaphor compares sleeping with death and waking with resurrection. Some people tend to take metaphors so literally that you are afraid to pull their leg – in case their leg comes off in your hand.

Third, time belongs to this world and not the next. In this understanding, which makes most sense to me, when we die, we pass outside of the dimension of time. When we die, we receive our resurrection body in the twinkling of an eye. From the point of view of a woman dying, there is no gap between her death and the return of Christ on the last day of the universe. But from the point of view of those who mourn her death and are still alive in time, then there is a gap, and so some texts in the New Testament speak of a future resurrection. Imagine your friend died tonight and the end of the world came in ten years' time. She would pass outside of time, and the instant she dies will be for her the same as the moment when Christ returns. For you who remain and mourn, there would be a ten-year gap between your friend's death and the end of the universe. So from the point of view of the person who dies, resurrection is instantaneous.

The resurrection is God's enormous 'yes' of vindication to Jesus. By raising Jesus from the dead, God declares, 'Yes, you are my beloved Son. Yes, you are who you claimed to be. Yes, the work you did was my work. Yes, you were right and the Pharisees were wrong. Yes, you did defeat sin on the cross.' So by the resurrection, God demonstrates powerfully that he is behind Jesus, in Jesus, and that he endorses his work and gives his seal of approval to it.

Before Columbus sailed across the ocean that we now know as the Atlantic, many thought he would fall off the edge of the world. But he got there, and came back, and our view of the world has been changed ever since. It was much bigger than many had thought. The resurrection of the Son of God changes our perspective on life and eternity.

With that resurrection, the future has leapt into the present, the promise is fulfilled, and creation will be renewed. The resurrection of Jesus has blasted a hole right through the wall of death. Through it we can catch glimpses of the life to come and through it we will follow him, for our resurrection is intimately linked to his.

Lord Jesus Christ,
we follow your trail,
  blazing through life;
we sail in your wake,
  surging through death.
We are your body,
  you are our Head,
ablaze with life,
  awake from the dead.

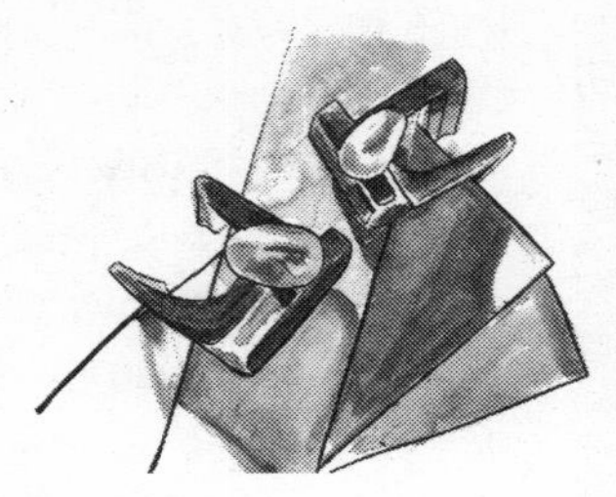

# Living

## PENTECOST

### Where is the power for life?

I was travelling on a train, on the way to speak at a Methodist conference on world mission, when I suddenly realized that something was seriously missing from the lecture I had prepared. I started looking for a work of art on my computer to illustrate the coming of the Holy Spirit. Somewhat worried, I did not come up with anything very satisfying – the usual doves and wings, etc. – until I considered again the photo of the 'Way of Life' sculpture by Jonathan Clarke, which was to be part of my conclusion.

Have a look at it. This is his 'maquette' – a small-scale first version – of his well-known sculpture in Ely Cathedral. The final version is 30 feet high and hangs on the north wall of the cathedral, immediately inside the west door. Jonathan designed it to be viewed from the bottom towards the top. The 'Way of Life' is a journey towards Christ. Unlike the final version, which has one path, the maquette has four interweaving, meandering, river-like paths within the one way. It is very evocative and resonant.

In my pondering about the Holy Spirit on the train, I suddenly thought how the maquette could be viewed from 'upside down'.

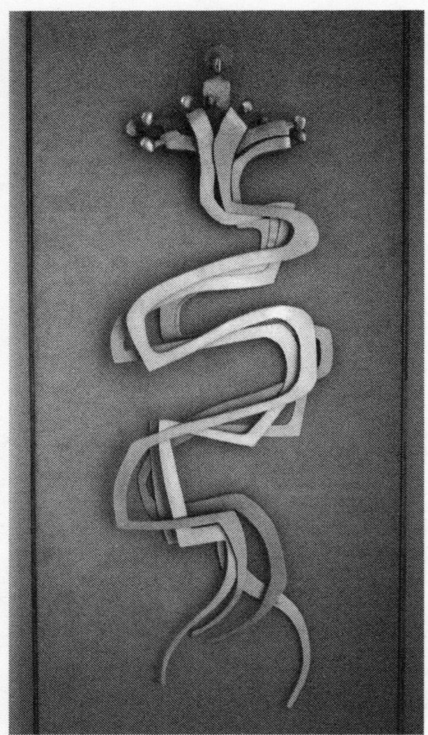

'Way of Life', Jonathan Clarke.
(See colour section)

Rather than a journey towards Christ, it becomes Christ pouring out the Holy Spirit on his disciples at Pentecost, who then travel on a journey outwards in mission in various interweaving paths. Intriguing and upsetting – rather like the Holy Spirit. So the same maquette can be viewed as going out and coming in, mission and discipleship.

A schoolboy was once asked to define the word 'anachronism' and wrote: 'an anachronism is something that could not have happened until after it did'. Well, you can see what he was getting at. John's Gospel shows clearly that the Spirit could not have come before Jesus had been glorified (John 7.39) – it would have been anachronistic – but Pentecost is the time.

'Pentecost' is the New Testament word for the Feast of Weeks, when the wheat harvest was celebrated by a one-day festival, during which specific sacrifices were made. This festival, 50 days after the Passover, also remembered the giving of the Law to Moses on Mount Sinai. Luke stretches language to describe this extraordinary event. A sound 'like the rush of a mighty wind', 'tongues, as of fire' appeared among them 'and rested on each of them'. As prophesied by John the Baptist, they were 'baptized with Spirit and with fire'.

Being touched with fire and being sent out in mission reminds me of Isaiah's vision in the temple recorded in Isaiah chapter 6: 'I saw the Lord sitting on a throne, high and lofty; and the hem of his robe filled the temple . . . the pivots on the thresholds shook at the voices of those who called, and the house filled with smoke.' The angel took a glowing coal and touched his lips. 'Whom shall I send?' 'Here am I, send me!'

The disciples spoke in tongues and praised God. It was this cacaphony of praise that drew the crowd, Jews from all parts of the Empire who were in Jerusalem for the festival. Luke is typically specific in his bubbling, tumbling, rushing, list of nations: 'Parthians, Medes, Elamites, inhabitants of Mesopotamia, of Judea and Cappadocia, of Pontus and Asia', etc. They heard the praise of God, in their own vernacular languages, about the great things God had done recently. No wonder they were amazed and perplexed as they saw this bunch of Galileans (from Galilee of all places) breaking the language barriers of Babel (Genesis 11). What can this mean? Others scoffed and blamed alcohol for this burst of enthusiasm.

Another schoolboy howler is the answer to the question 'What is the meaning of the word "bibulous"?' His answer: 'A bibulous person is one who quotes freely from the Scriptures'! In his preaching that day, Peter certainly does that, quoting from Joel chapter 2 and also from Psalm 16 and Psalm 110 – very bibulous, and very effective.

The following poem took shape as I prepared a sermon, the 'Birth of the Church', on this passage for St Mark's Harlesden, London, where I was a curate. This was after the birth of Miriam, our second daughter, in 1984. I wondered who the Church's mother was, how the disciples following Jesus on the road to Jerusalem related to the Church, and how the birth involved Good Friday and Easter as well as Pentecost. As a newborn child draws in great gulps of breath and then immediately cries out in all sorts of directions, so the newborn people of God breathe the Spirit and cry the word, upwards and outwards.

## The Image of Her Father

For many years in Israel's womb
The embryo grows, the Church of Christ:
First the Head, then the Body,
The Son of Man includes the many.

For hours upon a Roman cross
The Church's birth begins in blood:
Crucified with Christ her Head,
Constricted by the love of God.

The third day, from a gaping tomb,
The Church emerges urgently:
Risen again with Christ her life,
Released, relieved, the joy of God.

The fiftieth day, with tongues of flame,
She breathes the Spirit, cries the word:
Conceived, inspired with Christ, she grows,
The heir of all, the child of God.

The Holy Spirit may be called 'he' or 'she', but 'it' is not really appropriate, for the Spirit is profoundly personal, not a simple force. For a change, let's try 'she':

> She bubbles like a spring, tumbles like a waterfall, meanders like a river and welcomes us like the sea. You may as well try to bottle the wind as capture her. She is wild and unrestrained, surprising and unpredictable, yet true to her character and utterly reliable. She is reticent and reflective, giving glory to the Son and the Father.
>
> Like the wild desert wind she drives and scorches. Like the oil of the olive tree she heals and soothes. In a still, small voice she speaks and questions. The contemptuous proud she resists and brings down. The humble poor she supports and uplifts. Our imagination she enlarges and stretches. Our humdrum existence she enlightens and enlivens. Who can resist the draw of her calling to come to Christ and delight in God?
>
> She does not force and manipulate, but coaxes and draws. She inspires, enthuses, interprets and invigorates. She warns and reminds, convicts and convinces. She brings joy and delight, depth and sorrow, a feast in want and fasting in plenty.
>
> She does not ingratiate but delivers grace. She does not calculate but risks adventure. She does not rest on her heels but is fleet of foot.

She is not sedentary but agile, not ponderous but quicksilver. All who know her, love her, for she loves the Son and the Father.

As well as fire, water, wind and oil there are various other symbols of the Holy Spirit in the Scriptures. Paul's particular emphases are the seal and the pledge.

When a letter was sent in the ancient world, it would often be sealed with wax and the imprint of the 'seal' of the sender. That seal symbolized three things: authenticity, security and ownership. It proved that the letter was not a forgery; it meant that it would be kept intact until it was delivered to the person to whom it was addressed, and it signified the ownership of the letter. Paul uses this powerful image of the 'seal' in Ephesians 1.13: 'In [Christ] you [gentile Christians] also, when you had heard the word of truth, the gospel of your salvation, and had believed in him, were marked with the seal of the promised Holy Spirit.' So by receiving the Holy Spirit we are authenticated as being sent by God himself (see also John 3.33 and 6.27), protected till the day of ultimate deliverance (see Matthew 27.66), and assured that we belong to God (see Revelation 7.3–8).

Paul uses his second evocative image of the Holy Spirit in the very next verse of Ephesians chapter 1 – verse 14: 'this is the pledge of our inheritance towards redemption as God's own people, to the praise of his glory.' The word 'pledge' is a legal and commercial term meaning a 'guarantee' or 'downpayment', which commits both the giver and receiver to the completion of the deal. It is also more than that, because it is part of the gift as a sort of 'first instalment'. So we have been given the wonderful gift of the Holy Spirit, as a guarantee and first instalment of all that will one day be ours, when we live for ever with God. The kingdom of God has already arrived, both in the coming of Jesus of Nazareth and in the coming of the Holy Spirit at Pentecost.

In Luke chapter 11 Jesus teaches that the kingdom was both present and still to come in all its fullness. Jesus said, 'But if it is by the finger of God that I cast out the demons, then the kingdom of God has come to you' (Luke 11.20), and also encouraged his disciples to pray 'your kingdom come' (Luke 11.2). As a young Christian I sometimes used to wonder, 'It was all right for the disciples to accept that the kingdom was present because they had Jesus there among them, but what about us now that he has returned to his Father?' Did the kingdom come, then go away again, but will come back at the end of time? It seemed that the presence of the kingdom breaking into life in this world was understandable when Jesus was around Palestine, but how on earth did that 'presence' continue after his ascension to heaven?

The clue came to me through reading Acts chapter 1. The disciples asked a question about the kingdom (they really still didn't get it in spite of everything, and still thought it referred only to Israel) and Jesus replied with an answer about the Holy Spirit. This is typical of Jesus – ask him a generalized question and he will reply about a deeper issue concerning you:

> So when they had come together, they asked him, 'Lord, is this the time when you will restore the kingdom to Israel?' He replied, 'It is not for you to know the times or periods that the Father has set by his own authority. But you will receive power when the Holy Spirit has come upon you; and you will be my witnesses in Jerusalem, in all Judea and Samaria, and to the ends of the earth.' (Acts 1.6–8)

So the presence of the kingdom of God continues on earth by the presence of the Holy Spirit. The kingdom of God and the Spirit of God are therefore inextricably linked and both flow outwards in mission – the joy of passing on, and being, the good news of the kingdom in the power of the Spirit.

What about the charismatic gifts of the Spirit and the nourishing fruit of the Spirit? How are they related and who has them? Well, the body of Christ – the whole Church – has them. Everyone who believes in Christ has the Holy Spirit (Romans 8) and is called to be filled again and again (Ephesians 5). The famous evangelist D. L. Moody was once asked, 'Are you full of the Spirit?' He replied, 'Yes, but I leak.'

Being full of the Spirit does not involve wearing a perpetual grin – which tends to hurt the bearer as well as the observer – but peace in heart and mind, a surprising love of the unlovely, a joy in worship, and an overflow of service. We are filled again by God's Spirit in various places and times. I remember being prayed for at a church in Hainault,

Essex and not much seemed to happen. Then the following week, after reading a book in my student room by myself, I was so overwhelmed by the love of God that I could not express that praise in English. The gift of tongues bubbled out and deeper worship was released. Now not every Christian has the gift of tongues (1 Corinthians 12.30) because clearly not each person has *every* gift of the Spirit. The varied gifts include the speaking of wisdom, and of knowledge, faith, healing, miracles, prophecy, discernment of spirits, tongues and interpretation of tongues (1 Corinthians 12.8–10).

Spiritual gifts are allocated to each Christian individually as the Spirit chooses (1 Corinthians 12.11), but all are called to 'pursue love and strive for the spiritual gifts' (1 Corinthians 14.1). In these two verses, Paul provides us with a wonderful balance. We ask and the Spirit chooses. We don't just wait, but the choice is not up to us – thank goodness. In the chapter in between, 1 Corinthians 13, Paul describes the priority of love, which is the context for this balance.

Love is the first of the fruits of the Holy Spirit listed by Paul in Galatians chapter 5, where he describes the counteraction of the works of the flesh and the fruit of the Spirit. 'Fruit' contrasts with 'works' and 'Spirit' with 'flesh'. 'Fruit' is singular not plural, grows naturally, and is fed by the nourishment of the tree. 'Works' are plural and follow on from the focus on the flesh. In Galatians 5.19–21, Paul lists 15 examples of works of the flesh. Three refer to sexual morality ('fornication, impurity and licentiousness'), two to religious worship ('idolatry and sorcery'), two to intoxication ('drunkenness and carousing'), and seven to relationship problems ('enmities, strife, jealousy, anger, quarrels, dissensions and factions').

By contrast, Paul lists the ninefold fruit of the Spirit in verses 22–23, which are: 'love, joy, peace, patience, kindness, generosity, faithfulness, gentleness and self-control'. Intriguingly, they describe a portrait of Jesus of Nazareth, for he was the complete man, who was full of the Spirit. Following Christ, and being full of the Spirit, exercising the gifts and living the fruit, all interweave together and bring glory to God.

The Holy Spirit blows through the windows of stuffy offices, upturns neat papers on the desk, and reveals hidden letters that have been lost. Those who try to shut the windows, beware.

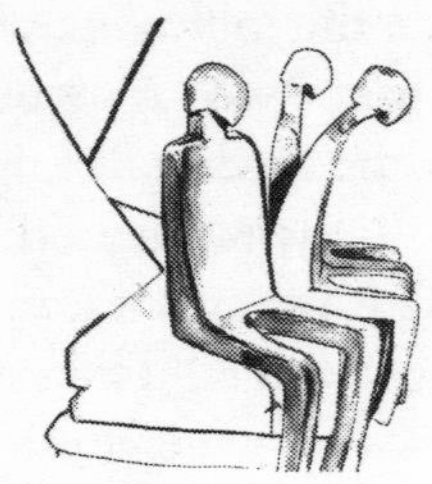

# Identifying

## TRINITY

### How do we respond to love?

The motto of a well-known British chain of shops is 'never knowingly undersold'. For many people, the doctrine of the Holy Trinity is never knowingly understood.

In Alan Bennett's play *Forty Years On*, when a schoolboy admits that he is still a bit hazy about the Trinity, his schoolmaster answers: 'Three in one, one in three, perfectly straightforward. Any doubts about that, see your maths master.' Now, in fact, maths is complicated in this instance, for here one plus one plus one equals – well, one.

The season of Trinity begins one week after Pentecost. This mystery of the Holy Trinity will only be unfolded in eternity, but there are glimpses of its meaning that we may see now. It is not so much accurate maths as spectacular theology. I mean 'spectacular' in terms of appealing to the eye – visionary – not speculative in terms of a tentative theory. We read of Isaiah's vision of God in Isaiah chapter 6: 'In the year that King Uzziah died, I saw the Lord, sitting on a throne, high and lofty; and the hem of his robe filled the temple.' Isaiah is caught up in the sheer majesty and glory of God. He knew God as One, 'Hear, O Israel: the LORD is our God, the LORD alone'

(Deuteronomy 6.4). Only later, with the coming of Jesus of Nazareth and the pouring out of the Spirit, did the writers of the New Testament have to respond to the eternal reality of God as three in one. Only later still did the theologians of the early Church develop the full doctrine of the Trinity, reflecting God who is majestic, yet so fully involved in his world that he becomes part of his world and still infuses it with his very being.

Grace Davie, in her book *Religion in Britain since 1945*, relates a fascinating response to her questionnaire:

> Do you believe in God?
> Yes.
> Do you believe in a God who can change the course of events on earth?
> No, just the ordinary one.

Now it is the 'ordinary god' whom most people think is boring, and so do I. But the true God, Father, Son and Holy Spirit is extraordinary and spectacular. In recovering the dynamic vitality of the doctrine of the Trinity, recent theology has shown that God is not so much incoherent as co-inherent. This means that the Father, Son and Holy Spirit interweave with one another. They are braided together, which is the root meaning of the word 'context'. The interweaving of Father, Son and Holy Spirit is the very shape of God. But this shape is also outgoing and, in a sense, centrifugal, spiralling outwards. God, in his very being, is 'missionary'.

Eternally, the Son has been coming out from the Father, and the Spirit has been proceeding from the Father and the Son, and together is worshipped and glorified. In time and space, the Father sent the Son and continually sends his Holy Spirit. Even the song of the seraphim in the Temple links the holiness of God with the whole world: 'Holy, Holy, Holy is the Lord God of Hosts. The whole earth is full of his glory.' The holiness of God is never locked inwards, but is spilling outwards to the whole world.

Isaiah goes on to say, 'Woe is me, I am lost, for I am a man of unclean lips, and I live among a people of unclean lips.' As we saw in the last chapter, one of the seraphim flew with a glowing coal from the altar and touched his lips. Having been cleansed, he was sent: 'Then I heard the voice of the Lord saying, "Whom shall I send, and who will go for us?" Then I said, "Here am I; send me!"' Once we are cleansed, then we are caught up within the sending, missionary, centrifugal, dynamic being of God, and we ourselves are sent.

This being sent – this mission – reflects the holiness of God in its holistic extent. Evangelism, compassion and justice are all three parts of the one mission of God. Some have tried to emphasize one at the expense of the others, but all three are one. Sharing the good news of Christ, being earthed in acts of mercy, and struggling with the structures of the world are all one. The three interweave, interpenetrate and bring glory to one another. So the braiding together in the heart of God – Father, Son and Holy Spirit – is also a spectacular image of holistic mission.

In Chapter 6 we looked at a painting by Silvia Dimitrova. In 2007, Silvia had an exhibition of her modern paintings and traditional icons in the Bishop's Palace at Wells, Somerset, and I combined a retreat with a visit to the preview. The following morning I returned to the gallery and meditated on the icon 'Jesus Christ, Saviour and Giver of Life'. Have a look at it, and then read the poem that I wrote in the gallery that day.

'Jesus Christ, Saviour and Giver of Life', Silvia Dimitrova. (See colour section)

## Gallery into Oratory

East Gallery, Bishop's Palace, Wells;
windows of light, in and on three walls.

At the previous evening's preview,
people gathered without gathering,
and looked without seeing.

In the peace of a fresh morning,
the gallery becomes oratory,
flowing with your presence.

I bring a chair to sit
and gaze, amazed, at you,
the Saviour and Giver of Life.

I peer through wood and tempera
to you, the Peerless One.
You see through my appearances,
and pierce flesh and temperament.

Your right hand gives
the sign of bread and blessing;
your left hand holds
the Word of life and love.

To you, I give thanks for saving me;
to you, I turn and return my life.

Though icons are unsigned,
Silvia's love for you
shines through and through.

She is the woman who
wipes the hair of her brush

on your face and neck,
your hands and garments,
pouring out her life.

Signing the invoice,
my inner voice sighs:
Pearl without Price,
owning nothing, I owe everything
to you, the Only One.

Through the abundance of your face,
flow the subtleties of your grace,
knowing, guiding, anointing,
searching, guarding, sending.

There were two surprising moments during my meditation in the gallery. One was when I realized that the icon I was contemplating was actually a two-way window, and that Christ was also viewing me, with his penetrative gaze. The other was suddenly seeing Silvia as Mary Magdalene. It was only later that I realized it was actually Mary Magdalene's day, 22 July 2007.

But why choose an icon of Christ to illustrate a chapter on the Trinity? Well, we can't get 'around the back of Jesus' to see God the Father. As we see Jesus, so we see the Father. There is not a mysterious dark secret, hidden behind Jesus. Jesus is the secret open to everyone. 'Whoever has seen me has seen the Father' (John 14.9). Jesus links his being and actions in love and mission with his Father. 'As the Father has loved me, so I have loved you' (John 15.9) and 'as the Father sent me, so I send you.' (John 20.20).

We can't get 'around the side of Jesus' to see God the Holy Spirit. God's Spirit shines through Jesus. The Holy Spirit is not wider or vaguer than Jesus. The Spirit of Christ is the Spirit of God (Romans 8.9) and interweaves between the Son and the Father. Perhaps in this icon of Christ, the Father and the Spirit may also be seen as present. The translucence of the Spirit seems to emanate from the face of Christ and we may hear the voice of the delighted Father, in an echo of the baptism of Jesus, 'This is my Son, the Beloved, with whom I am well pleased' (Matthew 3.17).

So what is involved in the doctrine of the Holy Trinity? Clearly, it does not mean that there are three Gods – as some Muslims claim that Christians believe. There can't be. 'Gods' is not the plural of 'God', for God has no plural. God is One. So if the three – Father, Son and Holy Spirit – are not gods, then what are they in their threeness? They are 'Persons' of the Trinity. Not persons as in separate 'people', but 'Persons' in that they are distinctively personal. God is not just one undifferentiated monolith, but one God in three distinct, but related, personal beings. They are involved in one another's work, they co-inhere. God the Father creates, and creation is through the Son and in the Spirit. The Spirit draws people to Christ to worship the Father. Christ, empowered by the Spirit, proclaims the kingdom of God and dies for the sins of the world, offering his whole life to his Father.

How did the concept of the Trinity develop? It came out of worship, study of the Scriptures and hard thinking and debate. Delight in the eternal divinity of the Son and of the Spirit, as well as of the Father, combined with the recognition that it was not right for Christians to say certain things about God. God the Father did not die on the cross. The Holy Spirit did not take flesh. God the Son did not pray to himself when he prayed in the garden of Gethsemane.

A key factor in all of this was that only God should be praised and worshipped. Anything or anyone that is not God should not be glorified in worship. The first Christians daringly began to link the name of Christ with God – 'to the one seated on the throne and to the Lamb be blessing and honour and glory and might' (Revelation 5.13). They began to reapply quotations about 'the Lord' in the book of Isaiah to refer to Jesus Christ, a man who had recently lived in Galilee (Philippians 2.10; see Isaiah 45.23 and Romans 10.13; see Joel 2.32). They even began to include the name of Jesus within echoes of the central text of Judaism, 'the Shema' – 'Hear, O Israel: the LORD is our God, the LORD alone' (Deuteronomy 6.4; see 1 Corinthians 8.4–6 and 12.5–7).

I don't remember many dreams that occur during my sleep, but occasionally I get caught up in a sort of 'prayer-dream' during the day, in which a deep encounter with God takes place through my imagination. On a retreat at Hengrave Hall in Suffolk one year, I was meditating on Philippians 3.10, 'I want to know Christ and the power of his resurrection . . .'. The 'prayer-dream' was of seeing Christ and, knowing I was recognized and accepted by him, embracing him and fully worshipping him. Then the disconcerting feeling that I was worshipping a man flooded into me – and I knew that you shouldn't worship a man, only God. At that awful, double moment of recognition – worshipping Christ and then feeling I had done something dreadful – I slid down at his feet, confused. Christ then raised me to my feet, embraced me again, and said, 'It's all right'. Amazed, I continued worshipping him.

I also remember a figure standing to the side of Christ, whom I later thought resembled Dietrich Bonhoeffer, the German resistance theologian executed just before the end of World War Two. Recently, I had been reading some of his works. This figure, seeing me raised, embraced and worshipping again, said, 'You have seen the secret of the universe.'

That is the heart of our belief in the Trinity. The natural praise and glory we long to give to Christ is actually inspired by the Holy Spirit. It does not detract from worship addressed to the Father, but focuses it. The Father longs for us to worship his Son as well as him. There is no jealousy between the 'persons' of the Trinity – only jealousy about misdirected worship towards things and people who are not God.

As the first three centuries progressed, the Holy Spirit was also recognized as fully divine for the same three reasons: scriptural passages, regular praise and hard thinking and debate. At Jesus' baptism, the Holy Spirit descends upon him and the words of his Father declare: 'This is my Son, my Beloved, with whom I am well pleased' (Matthew 3.13–17). After the return of his disciples from their mission, Jesus rejoices in the Holy Spirit and gives thanks to his Father (Luke 10.21–22). His last words in Matthew's Gospel are, 'Go therefore and make disciples of all nations, baptizing them in the name of the Father and of the Son and of the Holy Spirit' (Matthew 28.19 – *name* not *names*, it is worth noting). Paul links the Spirit with the Son and the Father in passages such as Romans 8.14–18, 1 Corinthians 12.1–11, 2

Corinthians 13.14 and Ephesians 4.4–6. An early praise song ascribed glory and eternity to the Spirit, as well as to the Son and the Father, 'Glory to the Father and to the Son and to the Holy Spirit, as it was in the beginning, is now and ever shall be, world without end. Amen.' When some people questioned the divinity of the Spirit, the reply came from this song, as well as from the passages of Scripture just mentioned.

What did God do before the creation of the world? He loved. But who was there to love? This pertinent question points to the Trinity. Without the reality of the Trinity, there could have been no love, or response to initiative, before the foundation of the universe. Apart from God, there was nothing and love needs someone to love. Love has circulated between the Father, the Son and the Holy Spirit from all eternity and will do to all eternity. After creation, creation itself is drawn into that circle of love – not becoming divine, but becoming loved. A monolithic, non-trinitarian concept of God, such as the Islamic one, does not have room for love from all eternity before creation.

Is there a mirror of the Trinity within creation? Various suggestions have been made, but perhaps the most fruitful is the concept of the image of God. Most people think of this as an individual concept, but a clue in Genesis points us to relationships: 'So God created humankind in his image, in the image of God he created them; male and female he created them' (Genesis 1.27). We, in relationships of love, are the mirror image of the relationships of love between the Father, the Son and the Holy Spirit. Coming at the image of God from the prior question of a mirror of the Trinity, opens up vast avenues of thought. God is three in one, and so people are most in the image of God when they are in loving relationships with one another.

We have looked at identifying the Trinity and the 'persons' within the Trinity, but what about us? How do we respond to this open invitation to life and love? What about our own identity and identifying? If we believe in Jesus Christ, then we are enfolded in Christ and are drawn into the eternal life of the Holy Trinity in prayer, life and mission. It is not that we become God – God has always existed and so no one and nothing can 'become' God – but that we are adopted into this family life of God, together with countless others across the ages and across the world today.

In Islington, for the last few years, we have had an ecumenical procession on Good Friday along Upper Street, from the N1 shopping centre to St Mary's Church. Each year someone, in a green robe streaked with blood, carries the cross in front of all the restaurants and cafés, shops and pubs, accompanied by drums and followed by about 500 people – young and old, black and white, rich and poor. We see what Christ did objectively for us, on our behalf and instead of us. In the church, part of the service includes people coming up and identifying with Christ subjectively, being part of him. One year Miriam, my daughter, constructed a large artistic 'installation' of the face of Christ in red, white and black clothes on the green chancel carpet. At the end of the service, we all came up, picked up a piece of clothing and buried them under the Holy Table. We were burying not only Christ, but also our sins and ourselves in Christ.

Paul's two foundational doctrines came alive for us: 'justification by faith' and 'being in Christ'. On the street, we remembered that we are accepted by God simply by his grace focused in Christ. In the chancel, we remembered that we died with Christ, were buried with him and now live in him, in the power of the Spirit. This is our ultimate identity and destiny.

We began our imaginative journey of the year with questions about plans and a quotation from a wise man about 'hurry'. At the end – which in fact will be a new beginning – as we meditate on our life rooted in the Trinity, it may be worth reflecting on a spiritual principle that was formulated by the same wise man: 'what you are always comes out; what you project, rarely comes off' (Donald Nicholl, *Holiness*).

# Further resources for your Christian journey

## Advent

### To Read:

Robert Atwell, *Celebrating the Seasons: Daily Spiritual Readings for the Christian Year* (Norwich: Canterbury Press, 1999).

Tom Wright, *Surprised by Hope* (London: SPCK, 2007).

### To Consider:

Eco-Congregation: www.ecocongregation.org

Arocha: http://en.arocha.org/home

### To Do:

Go for a familiar walk around where you live. Look up high at the signs and sights above eye level, which are often missed.

## Christmas

### To Read:

Anne Richards with the Mission Theological Advisory Group, *Sense Making Faith* (London: Churches Together in Britain and Ireland, 2007).

Kwame Bediako, *African Christianity: the Renewal of a non-Western Religion* (Edinburgh: Edinburgh University Press, 1995).

**To Consider:**

Christian Aid: www.christianaid.org.uk
Tearfund: www.tearfund.org
World Vision: www.worldvision.org

**To Do:**

Review your income and the amount you give away each year.

## Epiphany

**To Read:**

Anita Diamant, *The Red Tent* (London: Pan, 2002).
Richard Kidd and Graham Sparkes, *God and the Art of Seeing: Visual Reflections for a Journey of Faith* (Oxford: Regents Park College, 2003).

**To Consider:**

Church Mission Society: www.cms-uk.org
Network for Inter-Faith Concerns: http://nifcon.anglicancommunion.org
Faith to Faith: www.faithtofaith.org.uk

**To Do:**

Seek advice and arrange to visit a place of worship of another faith.

## Lent

**To Read:**

Rowena Loverance, *The British Museum: Christian Art* (London: The British Museum, 2007).
Nicholas Wolterstorff, *Lament for a Son* (Grand Rapids: Eerdmans, 1987).

### To Consider:

Bible Reading Fellowship: www.brf.org.uk
Bible Society: www.biblesociety.org.uk
Scripture Union: www.scriptureunion.org.uk

### To Do:

Go on a 20-minute 'prayer walk' around where you live, praying for the people you meet and the places you see.

## Good Friday

### To Read:

John Stott, *The Cross of Christ* (Leicester: IVP, 1986).
Mission Theological Advisory Group, *Transparencies: Pictures of Mission through Prayer and Reflection* (London: Church House Publishing, 2002).

### To Consider:

Christian Solidarity Worldwide: www.csw.org.uk
ReJesus: www.rejesus.co.uk

### To Do:

Watch a DVD of the film *Babel*, *The Passion* or *Kite Runner*.

## Easter

### To Read:

Alister McGrath, *Resurrection* (London: SPCK, 2007).
Rowan Williams, *Grace and Necessity: Reflections on Art and Love* (London: Continuum, 2005).

**To Consider:**

Lapido Media: www.lapidomedia.com
Church Army: www.churcharmy.org.uk

**To Do:**

Reorganize your regular physical exercise.

## Pentecost

**To Read:**

Alison Morgan, *The Wild Gospel* (Worthing: Monarch, 2004).
Vinoth Ramachandra, *The Recovery of Mission* (Carlisle: Paternoster, 1996).

**To Consider:**

ReSource: www.resource-arm.net
Alpha: http://uk.alpha.org/

**To Do:**

Pray with a friend for the renewal of your lives by God's Holy Spirit.

## Trinity

**To Read:**

Donald Nicholl, *Holiness* (London: Darton, Longman and Todd, 1981), latest edition 2004.
Tom Wright, *Simply Christian* (London: SPCK, 2006).

**To Consider:**

Transforming Worship: www.transformingworship.org.uk

Fulcrum www.fulcrum-anglican.org.uk
Covenant: www.covenant-communion.com

**To Do:**

Start a 'prayer photo album' with one photo per day of the month for someone or some group, you would like to pray for regularly.

# Acknowledgements

I am very grateful to the congregation of St Mary's Church Islington for all their support and prayers during my study leave, and in particular to Toby Hole (curate), who led the church during this period, together with Roger Tolson, Peter Scott Odusola and Steve Longworth (churchwardens), Liz Salmon and Ian Mylam (readers), Nick Adams (senior open youth worker), Michelle Liddon (pre-school leader), Lizzie Ewins (church youth worker), Wendy Holloway (parish office manager), Balazs Csernus (community development manager), Kate Tolson (community receptionist), and Tom and Barbara Quantrill (vergers).

I would also like to express my thanks to Stephen Oliver, Bishop of Stepney, for granting me the study leave of three months in the autumn of 2007.

I have greatly enjoyed the atmosphere in the British Library, London; the hospitality of Joseph and Jane Galgalo at St Paul's University Limuru, Kenya, of Moses Njoroge at St Andrew's College, Kabare, Kenya, and of Brother John at Turvey Abbey, near Bedford.

Some of the material in this book was developed for the Methodist World Mission Conference in June 2006, at Swanwick, Derbyshire, and for the ordination to the priesthood retreat of Chelmsford Diocese, in June 2007 at Pleshey, Essex. The comments and questions of the participants and ordinands were very perceptive.

Finally, and especially, I would like to thank my family for all their support: to Ali for her wisdom, insight and love over 30 years; to Ros, Miriam and Katie for their inspiration, questions and vitality; to my sister, Wendy White, and to my mother and father, Kathy and Ralph Kings, for their delight in God.

Thanks also to various publishers for permission to republish the following:

Bible Reading Fellowship, 'First Written Gospel', 'The Gospel of the Song', 'The Image of her Father', 'Turning Point', from Graham Kings, 'Poetry in Mission' in *Guidelines* (Oxford: Bible Reading Fellowship, September–December 2000).

Christian, 'The Gospel of the Song', *Christian* (January 1990).

Church House Publishing, 'Turning Point', 'The Gospel of the Song', 'By the Waters of Delivery', 'First Written Gospel' from Mission Theological Advisory Group, *Transparencies: Pictures of Mission through Prayer and Reflection* (London: Church House Publishing, 2002).

Churches Together in Britain and Ireland, 'Rabbouni', in Anne Richards (ed.), *Sense Making Faith* (London: Churches Together in Britain and Ireland, 2007).

The Christian Century, 'The Hostage Deal', *The Christian Century*, 7 April 1993.

Fulcrum, 'Matter of Great Moment', 'The Gospel of the Song', 'Rabbouni', 'Gallery into Oratory', Fulcrum: www.fulcrum-anglican.org.uk

International Bulletin of Missionary Research, 'Is Jesus the Son of Allah?', *IBMR*, vol. 14, no. 1, January 1990.

International Review of Mission,'The Image of her Father', *IRM*, vol. LXXX, no. 317, January 1991.

Lion Hudson, 'The Prayer Stool', Jenny Robertson, *A Touch of Flame: Contemporary Christian Poetry* (Oxford: Lion, 1990), p. 120.

*Highbury and Islington Express*, for permission to reshape my article 'Death by Water: Where is God?' from the edition of 14 January 2005.

Boekencentrum, for permission to reshape some material from Chapter 6 of my book *Christianity Connected: Hindus, Muslims and the World in the Letters of Max Warren and Roger Hooker* (Zoetermeer: Boekencentrum, 2002).

Bible Reading Fellowship, for permission to reshape some material I had written for their daily Bible reading notes, *Guidelines*, published in June 1991 (7.2, pp. 41–63), May 1994 (10.2, pp. 11–31), and December 2000 (16.3, pp. 136–53).

Anvil, for permission to reshape some material in 'The Redress of Mission', *Anvil* 16.1 (1998), pp. 7–11.

The Anglican Church of Kenya and Uzima Press for permission to publish 'The Kenyan Litany for the Environment' from *Our Modern Services* (Nairobi: Uzima Press, 2002).

The Archbishops' Council for permission to reproduce the Collect for Advent from *Common Worship: Services and Prayers for the Church of England*, which is copyright the Archbishops' Council 2000.

Citations from the Bible are taken from the New Revised Standard Version (Anglicized Edition) 1995.

## Artist credits:

Jonathan Clarke for 'Christ Blessing the Children', 'The Eighth Hour' and 'The Way of Life' maquette.
www.jonathanclarke.co.uk

Silvia Dimitrova for 'Rabbouni' and 'Jesus Christ, Saviour and Giver of Life'.
www.silviadimitrova.co.uk

Miriam Kings for the drawings at the beginning of each chapter, based on 'Three Figures' by Jonathan Clarke.
www.miriamkings.com

Aryo Pratyoto Kuswadji for 'The Indonesian Batik'.
www.batikart.co.uk/artistPages/special/special.html#apratSilks

Benson Ndaka for 'Kabare Library Carving of Mount Kenya'.

## Photo credits:

Rogan McDonald for the photos of 'The Indonesian Batik', 'The Eighth Hour', and 'The Way of Life'.
www.roganmacdonald.co.uk

Victor Virdi for the photo of 'Christ Blessing the Children'.

Simon Potter for the photo of 'Rabbouni' and 'Jesus Christ, Saviour and Giver of Life'.

Peter Stevenson for the photo of the portrait of 'Abdul Masih'.

Graham Kings for the photo of 'Kabare Library Carving of Mount Kenya'.

## Art permissions:

The Henry Martyn Centre, Cambridge, for the 'Abdul Masih' portrait.

St Andrew's College, Kabare, Kenya, for the 'Kabare Library Carving of Mount Kenya'.

Private Collection, for the 'Indonesian Batik', 'The Eighth Hour', 'Rabbouni', 'Jesus Christ, Saviour and Giver of Life' and 'The Way of Life' maquette.

St Mary's Church, Islington, for 'Christ Blessing the Children'.